MANAGING
GLOBAL
INNOVATION

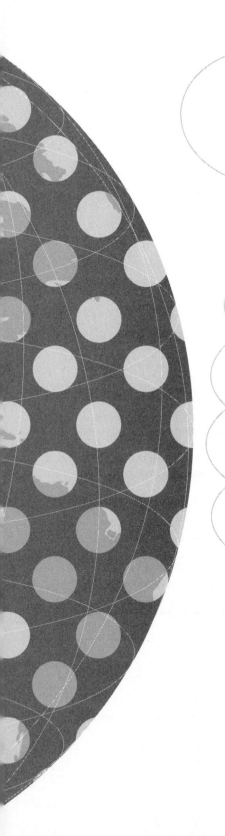

MANAGING

GLOBAL

INNOVATION

FRAMEWORKS

for

INTEGRATING

CAPABILITIES

AROUND

the WORLD

YVES L. DOZ   KEELEY WILSON

HARVARD BUSINESS REVIEW PRESS

Boston, Massachusetts

Library of Congress Cataloging-in-Publication Data

Doz, Yves L.

Managing global innovation : frameworks for integrating capabilities around the
world / Yves L. Doz, Keeley Wilson.
  p. cm.
 ISBN 978-1-4221-2589-2 (alk. paper)
1. Technological innovations–Management. 2. Diffusion of innovations–
Management. 3. International business enterprises–Management. I. Wilson,
Keeley. II. Title.
 HD45.D679 2012
 658.4′063–dc23

                                                    2012012904

CONTENTS

Part IV
Optimizing Collaboration
Succeeding Globally

TABLE OF SIDEBARS

In Memoriam
To Gunnar, Sumantra, and C. K.
They paved our way.

FOREWORD

This book explains how to conceive, build, and hone a global innovation capability that is enduring, practical, and rooted in the realities of both global competition and a company's particular approach to its market. Yves Doz and Keeley Wilson have brought their considerable expertise to bear on a subject of fundamental strategic importance, both rich in promise and perilous in its potential for misinterpretation and misapplication. Innovation has become such an all-encompassing concept and powerful driver of modern business strategy that company leaders lose focus when asked to define innovation and how they intend to achieve it. Globalization only adds to the challenge.

Along come Doz and Wilson with a blueprint for organizing, building, and managing a global innovation capability, from design through execution. And they offer seasoned counsel on how to tailor this blueprint to the parameters of a particular industry and the priorities of a given company.

Just as we do at Booz & Company, the authors start with focus. It is our shared belief that companies create long-term competitive advantage by recognizing, developing, and continuously improving a limited set of interrelated winning capabilities. Assets and market positions are transient. In contrast, core capabilities are sustainable and defensible in the long term. In the new world context of open market access and dispersed knowledge, managing global innovation will become an integral component in many companies' systems for growing winning capabilities. To continuously create and capture value, companies must not only know how to design and develop a valuable and flexible innovation footprint, but also learn to integrate worldwide knowledge and experience through effective processes and systems driven by strong leadership.

The notion that Doz and Wilson are onto something is not news to us—Booz & Company has worked with both authors for almost a decade, developing insights on innovation and how it has taken shape around the world, market by market. In 2004 we undertook a study of global innovation networks with INSEAD that provided a preview of some of the trends explored in this book, and we have continued to participate in their work on innovation regimes and global innovation in specific industries, such as telecom and pharmaceuticals.

Looking back just a few years, it is remarkable how rapidly our early findings have taken hold and become key issues for companies around the world, both in developed and developing economies. Our early study focused on companies from developed economies that were expanding their innovation footprints into China and India. In fact, that is where most of their incremental R&D investment was going. Now, we're observing a turn in the tide, as companies in China and India are investing their R&D and innovation currency in the United States, Europe, and even Japan. India's Tata Motors acquired not only brand equity, but also technology and a European automotive R&D footprint by acquiring Jaguar and Land Rover. China's SANY Group has opened R&D centers in Germany and the United States. Huawei Technologies has an extensive global R&D footprint and a $4.5 billion global R&D budget.

All of these companies now face the challenge of managing innovation on a truly global basis—identifying, accessing, stimulating, and integrating the best ideas and capabilities from around the world into innovations that will serve world markets while at the same time pioneering new ways of collaborating both inside and outside company walls. It's a daunting challenge, and few companies have found a winning formula.

Senior leaders need practical suggestions to find the proper architecture for implementing global innovation networks and meeting the day-to-day challenges of crossing borders in the development of ideas into products and services. This book is for corporate leaders but also for frontline innovators, and not only in developed economies, but also in China, India, Brazil, Indonesia, and other developing economies now spreading their wings on the global stage. It combines an understanding of the fundamental drivers of success in managing global innovation with practical strategies for building a productive and enduring innovation capability. It describes a long journey that requires a set of guiding concepts and principles, as well as an architecture of systems and processes. Doz and Wilson provide both in this expert road map for building the capability to manage global innovation.

—Cesare Mainardi
Chief Executive Officer
Booz & Company

PREFACE

In an essay arguing for a shift toward a more globally distributed and integrated approach to innovation, Sam Palmisano, the highly regarded chairman (and recently retired CEO) of IBM, cautioned, "As the twin imperatives of [global] integration and innovation render the old MNCs' networks of national hubs inefficient and even redundant, it is becoming increasingly clear that the twentieth-century corporate model is no longer optimal for innovation."[1] Similarly, at GE, Jeff Immelt has put the globalization of innovation at the center of his strategic agenda. During Henning Kagermann's tenure as CEO of SAP, when asked by one of the authors what he considered his company's most difficult strategic challenges, he answered, "To build a global innovation network." Along with many other managers, these executives have all recognized that over the past decade, there has been a growing need for radical change in the way their firms innovate.

As with any radical and systemic change, embracing global innovation will be difficult. It requires new structures, processes, tools, capabilities, and perhaps most important, new mind-sets. Our goal in writing this book, which is the result of more than a decade of research, is to give executives and managers from companies—both large and small, established and new—a guide to achieving that change and repositioning their companies to compete in the era of global innovation.

To explain the origins of this book requires us to go back to 2001, when Yves Doz and two colleagues at INSEAD, Jose Santos and Peter Williamson, published *From Global to Metanational.*[2] This was a manifesto for highly dispersed innovation, based on a few pioneering firms that were tapping the world for new knowledge. Although *From Global to Metanational* described what this new form of innovation looked like, it didn't explain how firms could build the structures, mechanisms, and processes needed to undertake dispersed innovation.

The magnitude of the challenge facing firms in building and managing a global innovation capability began to emerge in the fall of 2002 at a forum we organized at INSEAD for senior executives from leading global companies. By the end of the three-day event, we were left in no doubt of the genuine need for a deeper understanding of how firms could become global innovators.

Over subsequent years, our quest to understand how companies can build an effective innovation network and manage global innovation led us to conduct field research at forty-seven companies around the world, including Citibank, HP, Hitachi, IBM, Infosys, Intel, LG Electronics, Novartis, Philips, Samsung, Schneider Electric, Siemens, Toshiba, Vodafone, and Xerox. In 2004, with our field research ongoing, we teamed up with Booz & Company (then Booz Allen Hamilton) in a joint research agenda to gain a better understanding of global innovation footprints. We jointly conducted in-depth field research into innovation footprints in a number of sectors, but the centerpiece of our collaboration was a survey, "Innovation: Is Global the Way Forward?" This survey was completed by 186 companies from 19 countries and 17 different sectors, with an annual innovation spend of more than U.S.$78 billion.[3] Throughout our research and theory-building process, we have been able to hold various symposia bringing together executives from global companies as sounding boards and intellectual sparring partners.

In the past few years, the relevance and urgency of successfully implementing global innovation has intensified and the need for a book addressing the "how" aspect has become urgent. This book draws together the findings, observations, and managerial lessons arising from our research. Our hope is that it provides stimulating ideas as well as practical guidance for senior executives to strategically approach the configuration and deployment of innovation activities. For managers working in innovation-related functions, we have provided the frameworks and tools to support the coordination of global innovation and to maximize the benefits and minimize the costs of managing a global innovation network. Although we researched dispersed service, business model, and product innovations, we found the same lessons holding true for all. For illustrative purposes in the book we have mainly used the latter, simply because the innovation is more tangible and therefore clearer for descriptive purposes.

The book is divided into four parts based on the core "managing global innovation" (MGI) framework. In part I, chapter 1, "The Innovation Challenge," we introduce the fundamental conundrum that innovating with complex knowledge is best suited to a colocated environment (the traditional model of innovation), but the complex knowledge needed for innovation is increasingly dispersed, so global innovation needs to tap into this diversity. We put forward the MGI framework as the solution by providing a model for globally integrated innovation. In the final part of the chapter, we look at the evolution of innovation footprints over the past three decades and reveal that, with key capabilities remaining at home, poor network integration mechanisms and processes, and adherence to short-term cost-saving strategies, most companies are failing to build effective and efficient innovation networks.

Part II focuses on the frameworks a company needs to optimize its innovation footprints. Agility and flexibility are key, given increasing knowledge dispersion, shorter cycle times, and the need for greater efficiency. An innovation network of traditional bricks-and-mortar sites is not only expensive to run, but is never going to deliver adequate agility and flexibility. In chapter 2, "The Optimized Footprint," we suggest a new approach to building a global innovation network, where a company uses bricks-and-mortar sites for accessing and absorbing complex, systemic knowledge. If the knowledge at a location is either codified or embedded, we describe alternative, more flexible ways of accessing that knowledge from a distance or via learning expeditions.

An optimized footprint still needs bricks-and-mortar sites, though fewer. In chapter 3, "How a Site Creates Value and Why the Size of the Network Matters," we introduce a dynamic framework for organizing bricks-and-mortar sites for value creation and assessing the usefulness of new locations for increasing productivity, contributing differentiated knowledge, or seeking new opportunities for radical innovation. The optimal size of a bricks-and-mortar network alters, depending on a range of factors specific to individual companies. In the second part of the chapter, we explain how strategic choices, capability constraints, legacy, and corporate culture all play a role in determining the optimal size of a physical network for creating value.

In part III, we move from focusing on the configuration of innovation footprints to the integration of sites. A well-configured, flexible, and agile innovation network that provides access to critical knowledge and competencies both internally and externally still fails to create and deliver value if that knowledge isn't shared and reused. In chapter 4, "The Barriers to Integration," we outline the four main impediments companies face when transferring and integrating knowledge: a lack of connection mechanisms to share codified knowledge and connect knowledge holders within a network; communication barriers between different parts of the firm; an inherent difficulty in moving complex, rooted knowledge; and organizational cultures that fail to promote reciprocity. Chapter 5, "Improving Receptivity and Communication," identifies some of the tools and processes that the firm can put in place to overcome each barrier and leverage dispersed knowledge in innovations that will build competitive advantage.

The final part of the book, "Optimizing Collaboration: Succeeding Globally," examines why and how companies need to mobilize their dispersed innovation networks around global projects and extend their reach and capabilities through collaboration with external partners. When the knowledge needed for innovation is dispersed, it's impossible for product, service, or solution development to remain colocated. Yet many firms have experienced difficulties managing innovation projects dispersed across multiple sites. Chapter 6, "Organizing for Global Innovation Projects," provides insight into why. We then present a framework to guide organizations through the entire global project process, setting out new structures, mechanisms, tools, and approaches to adopt in order to build this critical capability.

Sometimes it's not a local presence that a company needs to access new knowledge, but a local partner. In chapter 7, "Collaborative Innovation," we describe how the nature of collaboration with partners changes over the course of an innovation project, from open approaches in the early stages when the opportunity is evaluated to building an ecosystem for the diffusion of the innovation. For each phase of the collaborative innovation, we outline the key considerations in selecting partners and managing the process. In chapter 8, we propose an action plan based on the three dimensions of change.

The familiar model of innovation that has proved so resilient for so long is woefully inadequate for the current reality in which the critical knowledge for innovation is increasingly dispersed across a wide geographic canvas; firms must respond to the rapid growth of new global competitors; and the deepening financial and economic crisis in the West calls for effective and efficient innovation in all sectors. Unless firms change the way they innovate and embrace the structures, processes, mechanisms, and mind-sets for a globally integrated approach, they will face irreversible decline.

ACKNOWLEDGMENTS

This book would not have been possible without the contributions of a great many people. Two in particular stand out: Steven Veldhoen made a significant contribution to the research on innovation footprints and has been a valuable intellectual sparring partner and friend over the past decade; Peter Williamson played a vital role in the early stages helping us shape and sharpen some of our arguments. The research work of colleagues past and present, including Kaz Asakawa, Chris Bartlett, Robert Burgelman, John Cantwell, Sumantra Ghoshal, Gary Hamel, Gunnar Hedlund, Arnoud de Meyer, and C. K. Prahalad, played an important role in directing our research and informing our arguments. Many people at INSEAD made valuable contributions; in particular, Jose Santos and Mary Yoko Brannen had important research insights. We owe thanks to Anil Gaba, Ilian Mihov, and the R&D department at INSEAD for their continued support, to Ian Edwards for helping us fund the work, and to Jeanne Larson and Muriel Larvaron. Without the support, both financial and intellectual, of Booz & Company, much of our field research would not have been possible. To this end, we thank Neil McArthur, Georg List, Thomas Goldbrunner, Kate Gulden Pinkerton, and Georg Altman.

We owe a huge debt of gratitude to the many managers around the world who showed generosity and patience in sharing their experiences and insights with us. Although there are far too many to list, we thank each and every one of you. Particular thanks are due to Mark Bennett, Gita Gopal, Paul Herrling, Dick Lampman, Alain Marbach, and Jean-Pascal Tricoire for leading us into new territory. We are eternally grateful to Andrea Cuomo, not only for his infectious intellectual curiosity, but for introducing us to many interesting companies.

We thank the anonymous reviewers for their feedback and suggestions in relation to an earlier draft and also Charlotte Butler for her suggestions for improving the final manuscript. Last, but certainly not least, our heartfelt thanks go to our editor Melinda Merino, who worked closely with us to improve the clarity and flow of our arguments and who played the dual roles of critic and enthusiastic supporter so well.

Although so many people have contributed to this book, any errors, misinterpretations, and shortcomings remain our own.

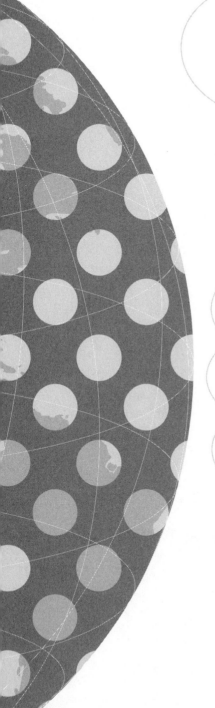

PART I

MANAGING GLOBAL INNOVATION

The Challenge

CHAPTER ONE

The Innovation Challenge

Every so often, businesses face a seismic shift in the way they operate. One of those shifts is currently underway in how and where firms innovate. Take a product many people use every day, eyeglasses. People with bad eyesight once had to wear glasses with heavy, thick lenses. Not anymore, thanks to the ability of lens makers like Essilor to access and integrate innovations from around the world.

One of us, who has poor eyesight, recently bought a new pair of glasses in France. After choosing a frame and giving his prescription to a local optician, he was told to return at the end of the week to collect the new glasses. Little did he know the journey his lenses would take: the prescription was first sent to a local division of lens maker Essilor for screening to establish the complexity of the lenses. This was then engineered in Germany by the Carl Zeiss Company (a partner of Essilor), which then sent specifications to PPG in the United States (another Essilor partner) to make the blanks from high-transparency polymer materials. From there, the blanks traveled across the Pacific to a Nikon plant in Japan (yet another partner), which put twenty-three coatings, each a few microns thin, on the blanks, including antiglare filters, photochromatic adjustments (so that the lenses darken in sunlight), and an antiscratch finish. The lenses then traveled back to France to be fitted and aligned to the frame, ready to be collected at the end of the week.

Essilor is one of the world's foremost corrective lens producers, a position it achieved by bringing together from around the world the leading innovators in their respective capability domains: PPG is a world leader in developing and making high-transparency light polymers; Nikon, with its long-standing leadership in high-quality camera lenses, excels at polishing and coating lenses; and Carl Zeiss is renowned for specifying the optical properties of corrective lenses. By integrating its partners' unique competencies in a global product-creation and manufacturing process, Essilor has built a strong innovation-based advantage.

Although our example's logic may seem obvious, it is a far cry from the way companies traditionally carry out innovation (for a detailed description of how the nature of innovation has changed, see appendix 1). Even before the recession beginning in 2008 forced many companies to reassess the effectiveness and durability of their innovation strategies, the need for changes to compete successfully in a rapidly altering world had become increasingly apparent. Whereas, in the past, it was sufficient for firms to innovate in their home market and disseminate those innovations across other markets, now innovations need to draw on dispersed and differentiated competencies, capabilities, markets, and customer insights from around the world. As with sales and manufacturing, innovation must become global.

The need for this change had become increasingly obvious during the decade leading up to 2012, yet few companies seem to have embraced it. The results of our joint survey with Booz & Company of 186 companies from 19 countries and 17 different sectors highlighted that, although the European companies were the most dispersed group, only 20 percent of their foreign innovation sites were outside the region. Less than half of the U.S. firms' innovation sites were outside the United States, while the companies from Northeast Asia had slightly more than half their innovation sites located in other parts of the world. Only 12 percent of sites in India and China were involved in value-creating innovation, while less than a third of foreign-based innovation sites as a whole made a contribution to core innovation activities. Few companies undertook global innovation projects involving multiple sites in their networks. This chapter focuses on explaining why firms are finding it so difficult to make the transition from local to global innovation.

Why Companies Can't Innovate Globally

Firms that have previously been successful innovators by creating one or two major innovation hubs in their home country and lead market aren't necessarily able to transpose that success to a globally integrated innovation regime. They have based their approach on an inherent logic of knowledge complexity and dispersion trade-off that assumes the only way to access and utilize complex knowledge for innovation is through colocation, and conversely, that a more dispersed approach to innovation is only suitable for and capable of accessing and integrating explicit knowledge.

The significant limitations of this conventional wisdom are potentially worrying for any company with an ambition to innovate globally: complex knowledge is critical for creating competitive advantage because it is context-dependent and can only be understood by familiarity with its context, making it difficult for competitors to replicate. A good way of thinking about the nature of complex knowledge in a more tangible way is to look at how chefs train. Most aspiring chefs need to acquire a deep understanding of the world's great cuisines, the philosophies that underpin them, and the techniques required to recreate them. Chefs can't achieve this by reading a range of cookbooks, because all the context and nuance critical to understanding a cuisine is lost in the codified lists of instructions. Instead, chefs undertake years of apprenticeships in leading restaurants around the world. Only by experiencing the environment and local conditions in which great dishes are devised and created can chefs truly master various cuisines and later transpose elements of them into their own creations.

Explicit knowledge, on the other hand, travels easily. In the seventeenth century, scientists all over Europe were able to disseminate new knowledge by publishing their research and observations. Now, explicit knowledge for innovation is typified by software development and testing in which teams in Asia, Europe, and North America work on the same project twenty-four hours a day. Figure 1-1 captures this knowledge complexity and dispersion trade-off, illustrating why colocated innovation is more feasible than a dispersed global approach when complex knowledge is involved. The problem and challenge is that innovations increasingly rely on inputs of multiple, dispersed, complex knowledge ranging from location-specific skills to local customer insights.

FIGURE 1-1

The knowledge complexity and dispersion trade-off

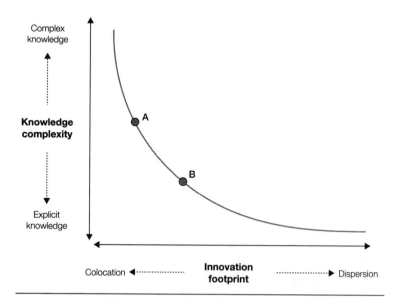

In the figure, the x axis represents the footprint of sites involved in innovation, from colocated innovation at a few sites on the left, to a greater number of globally dispersed sites on the right. Meanwhile, the y axis represents the nature of the knowledge required for innovation, from explicit, codified knowledge to context-dependent, complex knowledge. Currently, most companies are limited to innovation opportunities along the concave curve: because complex knowledge is locally rooted, companies dependent on this for innovation are forced into colocation, around the point marked A on the curve.

Over the past decade, many companies that have traditionally relied on a strong home-base innovation capability have faced pressure to access knowledge that is more dispersed, which has led them to simplify that knowledge. Take Infosys as an example. In the 1990s, as Infosys attempted to serve global customers with the advanced services and system integration and facility management skills it had developed, it implemented a global delivery model. In essence, it structured, codified, and standardized its knowledge so it could incorporate more sites into serving clients and facilitate the global integration of its activities. In other words, it moved from point A to point B on the curve.

But what if, instead of having to choose a position along the curve with all its limitations, it were possible to transcend the knowledge complexity and dispersion trade-off, or change the curve from concave to convex? What would it take to be able to access and integrate highly dispersed complex knowledge to deliver global innovations?

Building a global innovation capability that relies on complex knowledge will be difficult, though not impossible. As figure 1-2 depicts, flipping the curve to transcend the knowledge complexity and dispersion trade-off calls for new understanding, strategies, processes, and tools across three critical vectors: the innovation footprint, communication and receptivity, and collaboration.

To change the shape of the curve and overcome the complex knowledge and dispersion trade-off, the first step is to optimize the innovation footprint. This means being selective in both the choice and number of locations in which a company performs innovation. An optimal footprint is as compact as possible while still providing access to all the sources of knowledge needed to contribute to an innovation. Part II of this book introduces the frameworks, tools, and processes that enable companies to build an optimal footprint.

The next step is to improve communication and receptivity. Few companies have the tools, processes, and mechanisms to

FIGURE 1-2

Managing global innovation

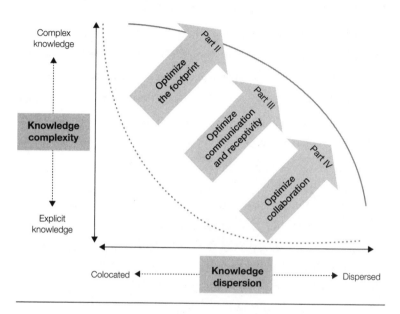

support the internal knowledge sharing and integration essential for a dispersed innovation network. Company cultures tend to lean toward original creation and knowledge hoarding, while few human resources policies encourage and reward the international experience paramount to global innovation. This deficit of integration capabilities paints a worrisome picture in which innovation networks comprise a group of autonomous or semiautonomous centers with neither the incentives nor ability to function as an integrated whole. In part III, we address the management and organization challenges companies need to overcome to improve communication and cooperation between dispersed sites.

Finally, effective global innovation depends on companies that collaborate both internally and externally. Unfortunately, collaboration falls outside most companies' comfort zones.

In part IV, we introduce the frameworks and processes essential for successful global innovation projects and collaborative innovation with external players.

In the preface, we mentioned Sam Palmisano's observation that a new corporate model is needed to optimize innovation. Some companies are already beginning to transcend the knowledge complexity and dispersion curve. They are building a new type of globally integrated firm that looks very different from the usual organizational models. For example, Tata Communications' footprint is designed to access the best knowledge around the world (see sidebar 1-1). It has a dispersed top team, reflecting the need to be close to critical sources of knowledge. It is able to leverage this knowledge by having organizational structures, processes, and a culture that support and reward communication and collaboration.

SIDEBAR 1-1

TATA COMMUNICATIONS: A GLOBALLY INTEGRATED MODEL

Tata Communications is a young, rapidly growing company. It is already the world's largest telecom wholesale carrier (selling capacity to other telecom firms). It has one of the largest submarine cable networks in the world, a Tier 1 Internet Protocol (IP) network, and an expanding enterprise business (providing solutions and services directly to large customers). Yet, in 2002, as the monopoly provider for India's overseas telecom services, it was operating in only one market.[1] By 2011, it had registered offices in 31 countries with 7,545 employees and 73 percent of its revenue generated outside India.

This rapid growth from local to global began in earnest in 2005 with the strategic acquisition of the submarine cable firm Tyco Global Network. The same year, Tata Communications acquired the Canadian voice carrier, Teleglobe. These acquisitions provided valuable capabilities and knowledge as well as a springboard for subsequent expansion.

From the outset, Tata Communications' proposition was intrinsically international, and although the company had originated in India, it didn't need to remain headquartered there. What made sense was to disperse the entire organization around the world so it could access widespread competencies and be close to important sources of market knowledge. Of the executive team, CEO Vinod Kumar, is based in Singapore; the head of voice, in Montreal; the head of data, in London; the head of strategy, in Mumbai; and the head of product and services development, in New Jersey.

This level of dispersion requires a strong emphasis on communication, collaboration, and feedback mechanisms. The company has invested in a raft of information and communication technologies (ICTs) to support everyday collaboration and communication between geographically dispersed teams, including Telepresence, internal social media platforms, and forums that supplement face-to-face meetings.

The firm sees unity as critical for a globally dispersed organization and central to its own culture. Every day, the collective culture is reinforced across the company by cross-location accountability. So, for example, a team in the United States may be responsible for deliverables in India or a team leader in India might take charge of a project in the United Kingdom. At a managerial level, the firm achieves unity through the constant need for collaboration and shores it up with regular face-to-face meetings. For example, the

(*continued*)

forty most senior managers meet three times a year, while the top one hundred get together at least once a year.

Tata Communications recognizes that not everyone is suited to working in a globally integrated organization. According to Kumar, "to be globally innovative, you have to let go of control and this doesn't come easily to most managers." Laurie Bowen, head of global data and mobility solutions, concurs: "Working in a highly dispersed organization can be chaotic. You have to let go of formality, be flexible, and focus on the overarching initiative." Consequently, the company pays a lot of attention to hiring people who will thrive in this environment. Most managers at Tata Communications have cosmopolitan backgrounds with deep international experience from having lived and worked outside their home countries and a genuine openness to new ideas and cultures.

In comparison to traditional organizational forms, a globally integrated organization presents much more complexity and places a greater onus of responsibility on every individual to adapt. Working in dispersed teams is demanding due to time and cultural differences, but Tata Communications has found that employees can find it an empowering and exciting environment. From a business perspective, dispersion gives Tata Communications significant advantages: it's able to innovate quickly by tapping its own expertise around the world; through proximity, it can build durable relationships with global partners and suppliers; and it is able to keep its finger on the pulse in a rapidly changing industry.

In some ways, Tata Communications, along with other emerging market global players, had a significant advantage over its old-world competitors. It didn't have a huge legacy structure and processes to overturn and overcome but was able to build a globally integrated model from the ground up. The journey for companies without that advantage will be much more difficult but no less urgent.

Moving the Innovation Frontier

Since 1975, after years of merger and acquisition (M&A) activity, there has been significant growth in both the number of sites where companies pursue innovation activities and the dispersion of these sites across a diverse range of economic and cultural environments. But most companies with dispersed innovation footprints have failed to capitalize globally on local innovations. At the other end of the spectrum, executives in companies that have remained steadfastly focused on the home base have hesitated to internationalize innovation for various reasons: the risks of intellectual property infringement, a strategically critical issue, are high; recruiting, retaining, and integrating good staff in unfamiliar locations is difficult; and choices about where to open new innovation units have become mired in indecision.

As outlined in table 1-1, globalization and the opening of new consumer markets; increasing technological complexity and convergence; demographic changes; greater external pressures and, in particular, environmental concerns; and offshore outposts and outsourcing are together driving a trend toward greater knowledge dispersion (for a more detailed analysis of each of these factors, see appendix 2). As this trend is more likely to intensify than abate, how well placed are companies today to meet these challenges? To answer this question, we will look

TABLE 1-1

Radical shifts forcing greater knowledge dispersion

The world then

- Traditional consumer markets in developed economies
- Specialization within industries based on discrete knowledge elements
- Locus of brainpower in U.S., Japan, and Western Europe
- External pressures limited to low-impact local regulations and standards in some industries
- Innovation taking place in the home market and kept largely in-house or with trusted local suppliers

The world now

- Large new consumer markets opening in emerging economies
- Increasing knowledge convergence across industries
- Locus of brainpower shifting to emerging economies, in particular India and China
- Growing external pressures with a focus on climate change and environmental concerns, resulting in varied local regulations
- Greater movement of parts of the innovation value chain to offshore outposts and outsourcing

at the results of the survey we conducted in conjunction with Booz Allen Hamilton (now Booz & Company), examining what current innovation footprints look like and what has driven their past and current configurations, the organizational structures and processes that support dispersed innovation, and the challenges these present.[2] We will then highlight what companies need to do to bridge the gap between today's reality and the requirements of knowledge diversification and dispersion.

The results of our survey revealed that the innovation footprints of most companies are becoming more global and that this trend had been in progress for three decades, during which the share of foreign sites increased from 45 percent to 66 percent of all innovation sites. Although using different methodology, other surveys were conducted around the same time, and subsequently all concurred with our headline findings that innovation footprints are expanding.[3] The headlines were interesting, but the detail revealed that the dispersion phenomenon is much more nuanced.

Some Sectors Are More Dispersed Than Others

To a great extent, a company's innovation footprint has been a function of the sector it is in. Industries that have historically experienced high levels of M&A activity or those whose products have been subject to strong local variation demands tend to have more dispersed footprints. So, for example, given that in the past there were extremely high levels of local variation in cars and trucks (catering to different safety standards, consumption concerns, price points, and local branding), the automotive industry understandably ranked as the most dispersed sector in our survey. The chemicals sector, which has had very high levels of M&A activity over the past twenty years, was also highly dispersed. As was the electronics industry, although we can trace the roots of its dispersion to the need to combine product innovation from the West with process innovation in Japan. It's worth noting that in all of these sectors, the knowledge base is codified, and because this type of knowledge, captured in mathematics and the scientific lexicon, travels well, globally dispersed innovation becomes easier. In contrast, we found that sectors, such as consumer goods, pharmaceuticals, and health care, that greatly rely on complex knowledge had less dispersed innovation footprints.

Where a Company Is Born Makes a Difference

With some exceptions, there are distinct regional differences in the dispersion of company innovation footprints. We found that Western European companies had the highest levels of dispersion, although other European countries dominated with regard to their innovation footprints, with 80 percent of foreign sites located within Europe. Meanwhile, during the past decade the share of U.S. companies' innovation sites based in the United States fell by seven percentage points, although more than half of innovation sites were still based there. At the same time, the locations of U.S. companies' investments in overseas innovation are changing. India and China combined are on the brink of overtaking Western Europe as favored innovation destinations for U.S. firms. Japanese companies fall somewhere in between their Western European and U.S. counterparts.

New Innovation Investments Aren't Where They Used to Be

In the 1980s, manufacturing migrated eastward and changed the competitive landscape for many Western companies. Today, the lure of India and China as locations for innovation is having much the same effect. From around 2000, the proportion of foreign-owned innovation sites in Western Europe and the United States declined as the number of sites in India and China grew dramatically. According to Booz & Company, between 2004 and 2007, the world's top–one thousand R&D spenders increased their total number of innovation sites by 6 percent and global R&D staff grew by 22 percent. But 83 percent of these new sites and 91 percent of increased head count were in India and China.[4]

These findings correspond with the predictions of future growth from our own survey. When we asked about planned future growth, we found strong evidence supporting a continued migration of innovation toward India and China, both in terms of new sites and head count. Perhaps more striking was the response to our question asking where companies would choose to open or scale up existing sites to achieve an "optimally configured" innovation footprint. The results, consistent across sectors, company size, and home country, revealed that 22 percent of all sites would be in China, with 19 percent in India.

Changing Drivers of Innovation Footprint Expansion

Is this shift toward India and China the result of well-thought-out strategic decisions with value creation in mind, or is it, in the words of nineteenth-century journalist Charles Mackay, the result of "extraordinary popular delusions and the madness of crowds," the modern-day equivalent of the South Sea bubble or Tulip mania?[5]

Over time, the drivers of dispersion have shifted, echoing advances and changes in other parts of the value chain as much as reactions to the external environment. What has remained constant is that the most significant drivers at any time reflect a shift in the underlying knowledge base. As figure 1-3 illustrates, where

FIGURE 1-3

The changing drivers of footprint dispersion

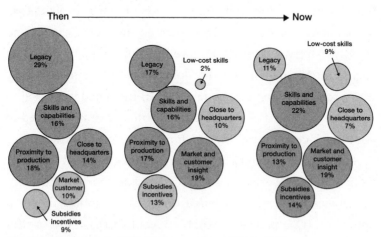

The first period is up to 1979, the second from 1980 to 1995, and the final from 1996 to 2005.

once the largest proportion of innovation footprints were "legacy" sites, a more focused approach on postmerger integration and rationalization has meant that the number of legacy sites in footprints has fallen. It was once very important for innovation sites to be colocated with manufacturing, but the digitalization and automation of production, together with reliable and low-cost logistics, have caused a decline in this once symbiotic relationship. Over the past decade, as products and services have become more complex and knowledge increasingly dispersed, the need to access new skills and capabilities has grown in importance to become the biggest driver of innovation globalization. Similarly, the emergence of new markets in Asia, Eastern Europe, and South America has resulted in the growth of innovation sites established to gain insights into new markets and customer groups.

Given that in recent years the number of innovation sites in India and China has increased dramatically, it's perhaps not surprising to see that the fastest growing driver of innovation-footprint expansion over the past decade has been the access to low-cost skills. But companies following a purely arbitrage logic have already begun to find the benefits short-lived, thanks to a combination of lower than expected levels of efficiency and rapidly rising wages. In 2005, a well-qualified engineer in India earned around half of someone doing a similar job in the U.S. By 2008, remuneration for the same job in India had increased to 65 percent of the U.S. equivalent and this trend is expected to continue increasing rapidly, reaching parity shortly after 2020.

The smart companies in our survey recognize that the gains from chasing lower costs are short-lived and instead differentiate developing markets based on other attributes they can contribute. Companies saw that innovation sites in China offer significant opportunities to access large numbers of demanding customers. India, on the other hand, attracts investment not just because of its large population of people with tertiary education, but because of the high quality of its scientists and engineers. Far from being a newcomer to basic research, India has created a homegrown aerospace industry and world-class IT sector, and developed the complex technologies required to be a nuclear power. IBM, HP, and GE, among others, follow this dual logic in India, with low-cost operations running alongside innovation centers that focus on leading-edge research.

To summarize, over the past few decades, the internationalization of innovation has both increased and changed in nature. Footprints are now more widely dispersed than previously, and based on the insights gained from our survey, we think that this trend toward greater dispersion will continue. At the same time, the drivers of innovation internationalization are gradually changing in response to the increasing dispersion of knowledge brought about by the radical shifts we outlined in table 1-1. But while footprints are certainly becoming more dispersed, is innovation becoming more global?

Footprint Dispersion: The Costs Are Accruing, the Benefits Are Not

Powerful global forces are rendering the technological and consumer knowledge needed for innovation more diverse and dispersed. On the face of it, companies would seem to be reacting well to this challenge, with ever larger innovation footprints expanding into emerging markets. But appearances can be deceptive. In fact, while a handful of firms have established new innovation centers for accessing knowledge to feed into a global innovation process, for the majority, arbitrage is still the core logic for investing in emerging markets.

The Arbitrage Argument Is Flawed

Despite India and China being home to 14 percent of all R&D sites in our survey, only a small proportion of these (12 percent) were involved in real value-creating innovation. The majority focused on low-end development support tasks, such as testing and verification, together with the adaptation of existing products and services (created in the West) to meet local market requirements.

This is a zero-sum game. Managers need to ask themselves how long this strategy will be realistically sustainable. First, these new consumer markets are growing rapidly and will require unique products and services designed to meet local customer needs, not just last year's castoffs that companies have adapted to suit lower price points. Second, wages are rising rapidly in innovation hubs like Shanghai, Bangalore, and Hyderabad, rendering any cost advantage short-lived. Third, companies will experience a dearth of qualified staff in developed markets, so it is inevitable that over time many more creative innovation activities will have to shift to where the brains are. It would surely make sense to begin building and integrating these capabilities now rather than wait until the tipping point has been reached.

Finally, the well-qualified and talented employees that companies need for innovating in new markets are drawn not only by good salaries, but, more critically, by the possibilities of stimulating, challenging work and decent career prospects. Just as their counterparts anywhere else in the world, in terms of Maslow's hierarchy of needs, employees in emerging economies need to attain higher levels of esteem and self-actualization to be fulfilled and satisfied in their work.[6] Innovation centers that focus only on repetitive, low-end work will find it impossible to retain and recruit the high-caliber staff needed for innovation. These people will choose to work for multinationals that enable them to make a valuable contribution, or for local entrepreneurial companies that will almost certainly be global competitors in the near future. In the critical battle for talent, which demographic changes will make more intense (detailed in appendix 2), those companies that have condemned their foreign innovation sites to low-end work will find it difficult, if not impossible to compete.

Just because the arbitrage logic that seems to be driving much current investment in India and China is flawed, it doesn't follow that there are no compelling reasons for setting up innovation centers in these and other emerging-economy locations. Both countries offer huge potential for companies to adopt cost-innovation strategies.[7] These strategies can encompass the leveraging of unique consumer requirements to develop new products with global appeal. They can mean adopting frugal innovation by finding innovative ways to develop products and services for lower costs without compromising functionality. Or they could involve innovating to build local mass markets. India and China's determined homegrown companies are currently stealing a lead by following a combination of these strategies. Instead of thinking in terms of arbitrage gains, Western companies need to play the same game and think of India and China as long-term, but big opportunities.

Key Capabilities Remain at Home

For every company that has embraced the real opportunities that a more dispersed innovation footprint offers, there are many more that are failing to exploit the potential of their networks and derive any sustainable benefits. While companies have increasingly dispersed innovation footprints, by contrast, most are focusing their innovation activities on the home base. Our survey revealed a strong tendency for companies to keep their innovative capabilities in their home market. Only 32 percent of foreign-based innovation sites contributed to core R&D activities. So, although footprints have been expanding, true innovation capabilities and activities have remained stubbornly close to home. Put more plainly, many companies are taking on the costs of an expanded innovation network, with burgeoning communication budgets and high management coordination costs, without building the sustainable competitive advantage that comes from an effective global innovation network.

Given the increasing dispersion of knowledge required for innovation, companies that have dispersed R&D networks but are limiting their innovation activities to their home markets are missing significant potential to create competitive advantage by accessing and utilizing valuable knowledge for innovation from their foreign sites. Of course, the reason that many companies keep innovation close to home is that their foreign sites genuinely have little to contribute. If this really is the case, and companies have innovation sites in the wrong places, then they need to reassess their innovation footprints so they are aligned with the knowledge needed for innovation.

PART II

OPTIMIZING THE INNOVATION FOOTPRINT

CHAPTER TWO

The Optimized Footprint

Most innovation footprints comprise a series of bricks-and-mortar sites. These physical sites undoubtedly play a vital role: they provide a colocated environment in which companies can develop complex ideas and concepts. They provide grounding in a local environment where companies can build and manage relationships with external players. And they provide the continuity that enables companies to amass and leverage deep expertise. Always at the heart of how companies "do" innovation, bricks-and-mortar sites have remained the default option when companies are expanding or restructuring their innovation footprints. But how close to an optimized footprint is this default option?

Far too many companies have discovered over the past three decades that building or acquiring physical innovation sites around the world has stymied rather than promoted innovation.

The networks are expensive to operate, difficult to coordinate, and rife with duplicated effort. The sites tend to compete rather than collaborate with each other. They are inefficient and largely ineffective.

Agility and flexibility are becoming ever more paramount for creating competitive advantage. As cycle times contract, there is mounting pressure to cut costs across the board and efficiency is key. At the same time, the knowledge needed for innovation in any given sector is increasingly dispersed across different consumer markets, industries, and emerging hot spots, and the rate of this knowledge diffusion is growing rather than dissipating. Against this backdrop, building new centers to tap dispersed knowledge challenges the dual mantras of speed and efficiency. This approach is not only costly, but will result in a significant lead time between the inception of the new site and its contribution to the innovation pipeline. The purely bricks–and–mortar approach is no longer a sustainable strategy for building a global innovation footprint. It slows companies down, limits the opportunities they can pursue, and places them in a reactive competitive position.

The solution to optimizing the innovation footprint is to build in agility and flexibility—to create something that is sensitive and adjustable to current and changing innovation needs. Achieving this type of footprint doesn't mean abandoning physical sites altogether. On the contrary, it means recognizing when they are the most suitable approach for accessing new knowledge for innovation and when alternative and complementary approaches are more effective. Whether a company is expanding its footprint or restructuring its current footprint, it needs to decide where to locate physical sites versus alternative approaches based on the type of knowledge it seeks. When the knowledge is complex and deeply rooted in the local context, then a physical site is probably the best option. But when the knowledge needed is more easily defined and transferable or explicit and codified, there are more effective and efficient alternative means to access that knowledge than sinking cash, time, and commitment into bricks and mortar.

In this chapter, we examine the pitfalls of an innovation footprint that relies wholly on physical sites and the causes of inertia that prevent companies from restructuring around a more agile model. We then describe each of the constituent approaches required for an agile footprint and the circumstances, based on the nature of the knowledge being targeted, in which each is best deployed. The first approach is a bricks-and-mortar presence that we call *experiencing*, in which companies access complex knowledge by being immersed in a particular location. The second, *foraying*, enables companies to mount learning expeditions to access embedded knowledge without building a costly, long-term presence. In the final approach, *attracting*, companies become magnets for explicit knowledge. The key to agility and success is having a balanced footprint and knowing when it's appropriate to experience, foray, or attract.

The Limitations of a Bricks-and-Mortar Innovation Model

Think of an innovation center in New Jersey, Shanghai, Basel, or anywhere. What probably comes to mind is a building filled with people conceptualizing, designing, developing, and testing products or new services. Close by, business development and marketing people contribute to the innovation pipeline by finding new market and business opportunities, seeking to understand latent customer requirements, and identifying embryonic trends. From the mature pharmaceutical to newer software industries, this conventional approach to innovation prevails. It presents a real impediment to flexible, fast-moving, and agile innovation.

Physical innovation footprints carry high quantifiable costs: sites can be expensive to run and maintain, communication budgets are high, and management coordination costs significant. But it's the hidden costs that really damage a company's innovation capability. By their very nature, these sites are immovable, which limits a company's scope for accessing knowledge to the places where its innovation sites are already located. So as new sources of knowledge emerge—with customer groups, new technologies, or centers of competence—companies reliant on a purely physical footprint can never be at the vanguard. But just think of the opportunities and flexibility available for companies that have broken free of this conventional approach.

Rolls-Royce, maker of integrated aircraft and marine engines, is a good example of a company that recognizes the limitations of an expensive, cumbersome global innovation network. The growing need for specialization and modularity in its leading-edge products prompted Rolls-Royce to radically restructure its footprint and regain leadership in advanced power systems. It replaced its physical corporate R&D sites by flexibly partnering with twenty-nine university labs around the world. It reviews the relationships regularly against output and changing knowledge requirements. This model provides Rolls-Royce with the flexibility to continually find and access the most relevant knowledge in the world for the development of its products. Unlike many companies, it isn't burdened with outdated innovation centers.

The argument against a purely bricks-and-mortar model is even more compelling with regard to opening new sites. With the growing dispersion and diversification of knowledge, most companies recognize that they need to expand their innovation footprint to access new customers and markets, capabilities, partners, and external experts. But it takes time to recruit and train staff and then integrate the site into an existing network. In some locations, particularly emerging hot spots, recruiting staff can be a particular challenge. For example, in places like Shanghai and Bangalore, there is huge competition for skilled, high-quality employees. When HP Labs opened its R&D center in Bangalore (see sidebar 2-1 later in the chapter), it took five months just to find the right local director who had the requisite experience in multinationals, contacts with local institutions, and scientific credentials to head the lab. Additionally, in some locations, there aren't enough qualified people to meet the demand. A McKinsey study of engineering talent in China found that despite large numbers of engineering students graduating from China's universities each year, only a tiny fraction were seen as good hires by Western companies and only 10 percent had the necessary social and communication skills to work effectively in a multinational corporation.[1] This recruitment problem is exacerbated in some places by difficulty in retaining good staff, annual attrition rates in double figures, and salary inflation not far behind.

Even after a company recruits and trains staff for a new innovation center, it still has to integrate a new site into an existing innovation network before the center can contribute. According to Dave Guidette, who set up new innovation centers in Mexico, India, and China for Schneider Electric, getting the growth rate of new sites right presents a challenging balancing act: "The new site needs to learn about products and processes and initially has to focus on low-end work whilst they build up competencies. At the same time, the best hires have to be motivated and committed. Developing codependency between the new and existing sites is key to the growth and success of new R&D centers. You have to create a 'need' for these sites and this doesn't happen overnight."

At the crux of the argument against an overreliance on bricks-and-mortar sites is the fact that locations seen as critical for innovation in a given industry today can quickly become superseded by another location tomorrow. Companies will be left with a network of legacy sites that no longer meet their innovation requirements, are expensive to run, and yet are difficult to wind down. So why are companies so wedded to their physical innovation networks? And why do they find it so difficult to restructure these activities? We believe they have fallen victim to what we call *footprint inertia.*

Footprint Inertia: Why Bricks-and-Mortar Innovation Networks Are Difficult to Restructure

We can easily attribute the failures of companies with ineffective global innovation networks to a lack of management attention, focus, or innovation strategy. But this view would be too simplistic, ignoring some of the unique characteristics of innovation and R&D centers that lead to footprint inertia or, in other words, the seeming inability or unwillingness to rationalize and restructure innovation footprints:

- *Social networks and relationships.* Much of the knowledge used in innovation is tacit and built up over time within and between small networks of people who have worked together on various projects and programs. While databases can capture and store codified knowledge relating to products, services, or solutions, valuable knowledge about why one solution was chosen over another, for example, or why a component was designed in a particular way is held by individuals and networks. Culling or reorganizing an innovation footprint can destroy or seriously disrupt these valuable networks, which act as the knowledge kernel for many innovation projects.

- *Retaining star performers.* Successful innovation requires a critical mass of talented scientists, engineers, technologists, strategists, or marketers, but every company has a number of star performers within its ranks who, by virtue of experience and/or sheer talent, make exceptional contributions. For example, when one of Intel's lead scientists, Dov Frohman, decided to emigrate to Israel in 1975, rather than lose him, Intel opened a small R&D center in Haifa so he could continue making a valuable contribution. This center eventually became a fifteen-hundred-person research facility. Many companies are reluctant to close innovation sites that are home to some of their star performers for fear they will be unwilling to relocate.

- *Intellectual property.* Whether via copyrights or patents, protecting core intellectual property (IP) is vital for the competitiveness of innovative companies. Many companies are reluctant to restructure their innovation footprints because it would entail closing sites in established markets where IP protection is strong in favor of new sites in rapidly emerging economies with weak IP laws and the very real potential that critical knowledge will leak to local competitors.

- *Hostage to home base.* Many companies have a sense (often real as well as perceived) of national responsibility or corporate citizenship to their home country. The news that a national champion plans to downsize or close local innovation centers often results in a national outcry not only at the immediate job losses but also at the resulting effect on local suppliers and subcontractors. For example, many global IT companies have been vilified in their national media for establishing large new R&D sites in India. Even though this hasn't resulted in direct job cuts at home, they have been accused of denying locals work in favor of cheap labor in the subcontinent.

Creating an optimized footprint will inevitably lead to the closure or downsizing of existing sites. Companies need to be aware of the causal factors or combination of factors to overcome this barrier. Once they understand the impediments to restructuring, companies can put strategies and mechanisms in place that will enable them to retain the positive aspects of their legacy network within their new agile footprint, while reducing the downside of a wholly bricks-and-mortar model.

Prior to restructuring an innovation footprint, a company should draw up a map of crucial knowledge networks. Most companies will already know the critical relationships within the innovation community, but a simple question like, "Who do you talk to when you encounter a problem?" quickly highlights networks of knowledge gatekeepers in any organization. These are the people and networks that the company needs to keep. But knowing who the gatekeepers are doesn't necessarily entail maintaining large physical sites. Rather, the company can formalize the gatekeepers' roles by giving them interesting, stimulating, and global work within the new agile network, either relocating to or liaising with sites charged with *experiencing* work, or taking on responsibilities within *foraying* or *attracting* activities. Similarly, closing a site doesn't necessarily mean the loss of star performers. A company can motivate people to relocate by offering more resources, greater latitude to publish work early, or the challenge of experimenting with new concepts in new locations.

Concerns over possible IP infringements and weak legal systems in many emerging markets will lessen over time as more countries join the World Trade Organization and the growth and development of homegrown companies in these markets lead to stronger IP laws and enforcement. Even so, many companies have found that the benefits (including new consumer markets, access to innovative suppliers, and talented and skilled staff) of placing innovation centers in countries that currently have weak IP laws far outweigh the potential problems.

Finally, a company may find it difficult to avoid being a hostage to a home base. Cutting jobs at home always leads to bad publicity, and more so when the jobs in question are at the core of the knowledge economy on which so many developed countries now base their economies. A public relations campaign arguing that the tax revenue from a company that is flourishing because of its strong innovation output based on an agile and flexible footprint is preferable to lower taxes from a company that is struggling to survive may soften the blow. But local politicians and media are unlikely to readily accept this. Instead, on this facet of inertia, companies will have to accept that the alternative is worse: doing nothing could spell long-term demise because the days of innovating primarily from a home base and shipping the results to markets across the world are truly over.

Achieving a Flexible Innovation Footprint

With regard to innovation, perhaps the most knowledge-based activity in the value chain, there has ironically been no discernible knowledge-based approach to organizing footprints. Companies have treated all knowledge requirements as more or less equal, perpetuating the bricks-and-mortar mind-set. But, as figure 2-1 illustrates, the characteristics and accessibility of knowledge vary greatly, from complex, highly context-dependent, tacit knowledge to explicit, codified knowledge. In addition, the half-life of any knowledge needed for innovation rapidly diminishes, while the number of knowledge sources needed increases.

An agile innovation footprint is configured to exploit the differences in knowledge types and ensure against shifting knowledge requirements. It enables a company to vary the mode of access based on the nature of the knowledge it is seeking (see figure 2-2). At the top of the scale is complex, locally rooted knowledge.

FIGURE 2-1

A simple typology of knowledge

	Knowledge type	Characteristics
↑ Increasing knowledge complexity	Complex	Highly context-dependent, systemic, exists in behavior and norms, can only learn by doing
	Embedded	Context-related, observable, loosely definable, accessible by seeing through different eyes
	Explicit	Codified, definable, transferable via common language or processes

This knowledge is held in norms, behavior, or cultural assumptions; the only way to access it is through shared experience—being there and learning through doing. To access this type of knowledge requires a bricks-and-mortar approach—*experiencing*. Moving down the scale, knowledge that is embedded in user behavior or technologies can be accessed without the need for a full-time, long-term presence via *foraying*. Finally when knowledge is explicit and can be codified and is likely to make a small contribution to the final innovation, the mode of *attracting*, which doesn't require any presence in the originating location, can be employed.

- *Experiencing.* When the knowledge is complex and systemic, and is impossible to attribute to a specific owner (either an individual or entity), a company needs to access it via a long-term presence on the ground in the form of an innovation center.

- *Foraying.* When the knowledge sought is technological but embedded in a local context, user behavior or some facet of how the technology was originally created often has to be understood. The knowledge needs to be accessed in situ, but this doesn't necessarily require a dedicated innovation center. Instead, small teams can embark on foraying exercises to see and understand the knowledge in its original context before translating it for use more widely across the organization.

- *Attracting.* When the knowledge needed is explicit, codified, and modular, for example in programming code, blueprints, and computer-aided designs, a company in a virtual environment can attract it. The knowledge needs to be able to move from its location of origin to the attractor company via ICTs without losing any of its integrity or meaning.

FIGURE 2-2

An optimized innovation footprint

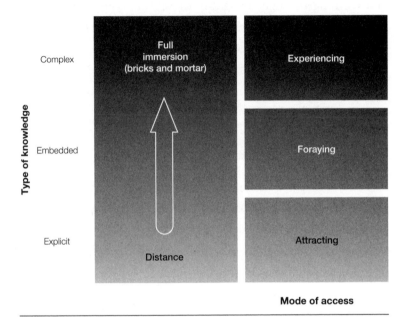

Experiencing: Immersion in the Local Environment

The limitations of physical innovation networks we have described shouldn't preclude the continuation or establishment of bricks-and-mortar sites in the future. The only caveat is that these sites are used to access the systemic, diffuse complex knowledge held in norms, social interactions, and culture. Only under these circumstances is an actual, physical site a viable option. Complex knowledge is locally rooted and deeply embedded. It is difficult to define and will invariably be very different from a company's existing knowledge base. To access complex knowledge requires learning by doing, seeing, and being there. It means growing local roots and cultivating local relationships, which can only be done by immersion in the local context or *experiencing*.

For most companies, the business rationale behind the need to access complex, locally rooted knowledge is to achieve growth by entering new businesses and or new markets.[2] For example, when the Japanese cosmetics group Shiseido decided to enter the global perfumery business, it chose France, the world's leading market in this segment, as a base. As we describe in chapter 5, trying to understand the subtle nuances of design, packaging, and marketing in perfumery from Japan was impossible. However, learning by doing, seeing, and being in France helped Shiseido develop the Issey Miyake and Jean Paul Gaultier brands, among others, that have had lasting success.

In recent years, a new phenomenon is the growing importance of low-cost, high-value innovation in markets where necessity is the mother of invention.[3] To participate in this growing field and innovate at the bottom of the pyramid, companies need to access complex knowledge that requires them to undertake innovation activities in situ.[4] Building on Tata's lead in developing a low-cost, fuel-efficient car for India's vast and growing middle class (currently estimated at over 100 million households), many auto manufacturers, including Suzuki and Hyundai, set up innovation hubs in India to enable them to compete in what the industry widely acknowledges will be one of the few future growth areas. Only by being on the ground and understanding consumer requirements and preferences, road conditions, maintenance, and servicing constraints can manufacturers come up with a radically different vehicle at a price point for those at the bottom of the pyramid.

Similarly, HP recognized that, although a potentially huge market, India was underserved, and by the time the economy had developed sufficiently for HP to sell its global product range (albeit pared-down versions to achieve attractive price points), local competitors would have emerged to make market entry difficult. To develop products and services that would be attractive in an Indian market, it needed to open a bricks-and-mortar innovation center (see sidebar 2-1). HP realized that it had to have a deep understanding of how people lived and worked in India and the challenges the government, the administration, and businesses faced.

SIDEBAR 2-1

HP LABS INDIA: EXPERIENCING VIA IMMERSION IN A NEW CONTEXT

In the 1990s, HP Labs began to recognize the strategic imperative in examining what kind of ICTs it would need to create a market in developing countries. It saw that most of HP's future growth would be in these markets and realized that most MNCs in developing countries focused on serving the tiny proportion of rich people at the top of the pyramid. But the greatest and most underexploited opportunities lay with the group in the middle of the pyramid.

HP already had an interest in developing economies with its emerging market solutions (EMS) group. Its role was to adapt existing HP technologies to make them affordable and usable in poor countries. But this approach didn't address the real opportunity of understanding the unmet and unarticulated technology needs in developing economies. The type of research that would tap into these needs had to be on the ground, immersed in the local context.

In 2000, HP Labs set up a new lab in Bangalore India (HPLI) with a dual mandate to develop new solutions and products for the underserved populations of developing economies and also "learn how to learn" in new, very different markets.

Building a management team to establish the lab with the right attributes, vision, experience, and connections to HP's businesses, head office, and local networks of contacts was paramount. Gita Gopal, who had been involved in the project from its inception, took on the role of the lab's associate director. But rather than being based in India, she remained in Palo Alto to provide a voice for the lab back at the center. The lab also hired an HP veteran to be based in India and to forge relationships with HP's global businesses.

The local director's role for the first few years while the lab established local connections and partnerships would be quite different from its later incarnation once the lab was up and running. So, initially, HPLI needed to hire a prominent local to give the lab credibility and provide an external network of contacts. It asked an executive search agency to find candidates who met some challenging criteria: they had to be eminent scientists in their own right, have business experience, and understand how an MNC operates. The search process took almost five months resulting in the hiring of Srinivasan Ramani. He had a long and distinguished career that included serving on the United Nations' high-level panel of advisers in ICTs.

The lab's approach to conducting research differed radically from the traditional approach that began by identifying technical challenges. HPLI's mandate was to understand the end-user problems that needed to be solved and to identify the potential of the market. The softer sciences, such as ethnography, anthropology, and sociology, would play a prominent role in driving the research effort.

Although HPLI focuses on creating technologies for markets that don't yet appear on the radar of the business divisions, it falls to the businesses to take those concept technologies to market, since HPLI has neither the skill nor the charter to manufacture and sell its innovations. It's therefore vital for HPLI to identify and adopt

(continued)

business sponsors for the projects it pursues. For example, HPLI designed a "script mail device" to allow people to send and receive handwritten e-mails via the telephone without the need for an expensive PC or other script-based input devices. HP's relevant business unit was able to target this device to institutional buyers. Similarly, when HPLI developed the "shopkeepers' assistant," a small, simple device that could track inventory, once the relevant HP business unit was brought into the project, it realized that trying to sell a single device to every shopkeeper would be unprofitable, if not impossible. But targeting large suppliers to India's 5.5 million independent retail outlets (and thus allowing them to track inventory in the stores they supplied) would be much more feasible.

HPLI is now a well-established research center in HP's network, with its own network of research collaborations around the world. Its research projects focus on the needs of users and consumers in the developing world, but many of its developments have a wider impact, such as simplifying Web access and using technology in education.

Any company can set up experiencing sites, but these will be successful only if the company makes and maintains the requisite resource and management commitments. To gain value from experiencing, the company should only make the commitment when the source of the knowledge and the nature of the knowledge it is seeking has some or all the following characteristics:

- *Diffuse ownership.* No individual or identifiable group possesses all of the knowledge sought. For example, when Novartis opened a research center in Singapore to focus on tropical diseases (discussed in chapter 3), the knowledge it needed was highly diffuse. Physicians who treated patients suffering from the diseases, NGOs headquartered in Singapore that knew about delivering health services in neighboring poor countries, and Singapore's own local scientific communities that had worked in these areas for decades held the critical knowledge. To learn from all of these different sources and then continuously combine this new, complementary knowledge with its core drug-development knowledge called for Novartis to use an experiencing approach.

- *Complex.* The knowledge is tacit, deeply rooted in the local context in a combination of norms, behavior, actions, mental models, or beliefs. It is not easily articulated and is very difficult to transfer to other locations. For example, the knowledge that enabled HP to develop innovative new products for emerging markets was complex: it wasn't possible by merely reading reports to understand the implications and ramifications of living and working in a country with an underdeveloped and unreliable infrastructure. Staff at HP had to learn by experiencing firsthand the impact and constraints on people's everyday lives and actions. Only then were they equipped to recognize opportunities to develop solutions.

- *Difficult to define.* Before embarking on experiencing, a company will find that the structure of the knowledge is unknown or fuzzy. A greater understanding of what can be learned will be revealed only through the process of learning. For example, HP Labs went to India to learn about the frustrations and difficulties of living and working in a huge, poor, and largely rural developing economy and to develop products and services to help alleviate some of these factors. A more precise definition of what HP Labs wanted to learn only began to emerge as it learned more about India and its people.

Foraying: Scouting with a Mission

Foraying is a flexible approach that is very effective and efficient for acquiring specific knowledge to replicate as a new product line or business model. By sending out learning expeditions to identify new embedded knowledge in unfamiliar places, many companies have been able to bring innovations to market before their larger and more powerful competitors.

Take the relatively small French aerospace company, Snecma. It was the first non-Russian company to design and manufacture innovative thermal coatings, lightweight welded feed pipes, and plasma propulsion engines for satellites. These innovations didn't originate in the company's French labs but were the result of foraying (see sidebar 2-2). Although Snecma's foraying activity began in 1990 when it sent a small team of scouts to the collapsing Soviet Union to look for advanced technologies that had been developed during its years of isolation, the benefits continue today. As Snecma's story shows, the best results from foraying come from being first and building long-term relationships.

SIDEBAR 2-2

SNECMA: FORAYING VIA LEARNING EXPEDITIONS

SEP, a small French space propulsion company (later to become part of the French government-controlled aerospace engines group, Snecma), began a journey in 1990 to prospect for new technologies in the Soviet Union. It didn't know what it was looking for, or who might be the holders of this unspecified knowledge. But it did have an inkling that the legacy of the Cold War space

---

race would add some radically different technological approaches to those then common in the West. This prospecting presented an opportunity for the small French group to gain competitive advantage through differentiation.

Through his work in helping set up the International Space University (ISU), SEP engineer Marcel Pouliquen had established a number of contacts in the Soviet space industry and in 1990 received an invitation for a small delegation from SEP to attend the Moscow Air Show.[5] From this initial visit at the beginning of 1991, a one-year discovery project was set up with the full support of SEP's president and CEO. An exploratory team of three would be given a mandate to find opportunities in the Soviet Union and develop relationships with Russian institutes, design centers, and producers.

SEP needed to select people for the prospecting team who would maximize the diversity extractable from the Soviet Union. They would have to have the requisite core skills for sensing, such as intellectual curiosity, a thorough understanding of the business, technology, and strategic requirements, diplomacy, determination and cultural sensitivity. They would also need to have technical and functional specialties and interests that would allow them to access and assess a broad range of new knowledge. Joining Pouliquen were Jacques Cipriano, an engineer who had worked on the engines for the Ariane space program, and André Giraudeau, who had a background in metallurgy and had spent many years as head of purchasing for SEP.

In early March 1991, the team arrived in the Soviet Union to begin its first phase of discussion and exploration. From his work with the ISU, Pouliquen knew a handful of professors and researchers at the Moscow Aviation Institute (MAI). This prestigious training center in

(continued)

the Soviet Union not only produced leading-edge basic research but, with around eighteen thousand enrolled students, educated most of the people who then went into the local aerospace industry. According to Giraudeau, "We were thinking on our feet. We felt as we went along. Despite the broad objectives, there was no master plan directing how we were going to work and how we were to achieve those objectives. But we had to start somewhere and Pouliquen's well-connected contacts at MAI represented the most obvious entry point to a wider network."

Once detailed discussions had begun in earnest, the SEP team recognized that it needed to build processes that would connect the Soviet and SEP specialists. It devised a system of workshops and small group meetings in France at which the Soviet engineers and professors presented their work, while groups of French engineers visited the Soviet Union.

After accessing a wide range of interesting technologies (from around eighty different organizations) and allowing SEP's engineers to familiarize themselves with them, the team organized rigorous tests to see how the technologies performed in terms of quality and durability not only in themselves but in the context of SEP's systems in which they would be integrated or embedded. SEP awarded fifty contracts for deliverables.

By 2011, SEP (now Snecma) was in the enviable position of having a considerable amount of business in Russia, ranging from joint ventures to design and manufacture plasma propulsion engines for satellites and the engine for the Russian Regional Jet program, to collaboration for landing gear and helicopter engines. What makes this level of involvement in Russia all the more remarkable is that, when compared to the giants that dominate the aerospace industry, such as Pratt & Whitney, BAE Systems,

---

Lockheed Martin, and Northrop Grumman, Snecma is a small player. However, Snecma is the first to acknowledge that all its current activity in Russia and many of its innovative products are a direct result of the relationships it built and knowledge it accessed through the SEP prospecting project two decades ago.

Foraying relies on a small team of people or scouts who go on learning expeditions to find and access new embedded knowledge in its original context. They act as relays between the source of new knowledge and the home base of the organization and are responsible for devising methods and processes to decontextualize and transfer the relevant knowledge. KPN, a midsized Dutch telecom operator used the foraying approach to introduce i-mode, the first successful mobile content platform, to Europe. The Dutch company sent learning expeditions comprised of young staff members from a variety of departments to Japan to work with NTT DoCoMo and observe how the Japanese used mobile products and services. KPN's scouts not only brought back codified knowledge in the form of special i-mode-enabled smartphones, but, based on their observations in the workplace and in bars and clubs, were able to explain to their colleagues in Europe how the Japanese used i-mode.

The success or failure of foraying activities primarily depends on having the right people in place as scouts (although there are other considerations, such as senior management support and a receptive innovation organization back home). Scouts need a range of specialist skills so that they can assess the value and usefulness of the new knowledge they find. But they also need to be generally inquisitive and culturally ambidextrous to operate simultaneously in more than one context. The task of understanding what is relevant and how to make it transferable lies with them.

The foraying access approach provides a high level of agility and flexibility. A company can mount relatively low-cost learning expeditions as and when required, with the new knowledge feeding into the innovation pipeline without the delays commonly found in the experiencing approach. Any company willing to invest in hiring and supporting scouts can use this method. However, for foraying to be a viable option, the knowledge source and knowledge the company is seeking need to conform to the following requirements:

- *Close to core knowledge base.* An overlap between the new knowledge and a company's existing knowledge base is essential. Scouts need to assess the value of the new knowledge and understand how it fits in its original context and how to transfer it to a new context; if the knowledge were completely unfamiliar, this process wouldn't be possible. Snecma, for example, was able to transfer some Russian technologies to France because what it had found in Russia represented a different solution to technology challenges and not knowledge from a different domain.

- *Focused but not too tightly defined.* Whereas experiencing allows for true exploration, with foraying, a company needs to have a broad idea upfront of what knowledge it is seeking. Too broad a definition of what it needs to find—for example, "Is there anything of interest in *x* location?"—is not be a feasible starting point because it places too much reliance on serendipity to yield any useful findings. Both Snecma and KPN were able to loosely define the knowledge they were looking for: Snecma wanted any interesting and useful space propulsion technologies developed in Russia during its years of isolation, while KPN wanted to understand the technical, social, and business model elements behind a specific mobile telecom product in Japan. It's not necessary to define a specific agenda at the outset of the foraying exercise, but scouts must have a general direction and focus that leaves room for discovery and learning.

- *Identifiable knowledge holders.* Before dispatching scouts on a foraying mission, a company must know which individuals or entities either own or hold the knowledge it is looking for, or act as entry points to the right networks of knowledge holders. For example, when the Snecma scouts went to Russia, they already knew some professors at the Moscow Aviation Institute. These well-connected people pushed the Snecma scouts in the right direction and made the necessary introductions.

Attracting: Being a Magnet for Knowledge

Greater knowledge dispersion means that new technologies or solutions can emerge anywhere. In contrast to experiencing and foraying, the purpose of attracting is to stimulate a stream of innovative ideas and new technologies to "beat a path to your door" rather than going out to look for that new knowledge. Depending upon how well defined the problem or knowledge gap is, there are two different approaches to attracting: the first, *focused attracting* (often referred to as "open innovation"), is the appropriate approach when the knowledge sought can be well defined; for example, when a component has to perform a specific function or a problem needs to be solved.[6] The second approach, *broad attracting*, on the other hand, provides much greater latitude for discovery, akin to trawling for potentially interesting ideas related to loosely defined problems.

Focused attracting, in essence, allows companies to post specific innovation problems to a wide network of people who will then try to solve them. Many firms, such as InnoCentive, YourEncore, and NineSigma, are intermediaries between companies seeking solutions to specific innovation challenges and problem solvers (which include retired scientists, entrepreneurs, university labs, and government research centers). For example, as part of its connect-and-develop strategy, Procter & Gamble regularly seeks solutions to innovation problems by focused attracting. By 2011, Procter & Gamble's focused attracting resulted in over one thousand agreements, either outbound or inbound, across a wide range of areas including technology, design, marketing, and research methods. Critical to the success of focused attracting is having a very well-defined knowledge gap for which "you know what you don't know."

While focused attracting is very democratic, with any company able to engage the services of a knowledge-search intermediary company, not all companies can undertake broad attracting. In this scenario, knowledge holders seek out the recipient company as a potential receptacle for their innovation or contribution. Prominent companies automatically attract external ideas, but in order to stimulate an inflow of new knowledge, firms can publish their broad areas of research interest (with the added benefit of focusing the incoming flow of knowledge). The obvious benefits are that for little cost, both in financial and manpower resources and time, a company can access and assess a huge number of new technologies and ideas. The potential downside is that the external knowledge sought confirms rather than challenges a firm's strategic choices, and it may miss disruptive innovations.

Although Nokia has recently lost its platform and industry leadership because it stuck with the Symbian operating system instead of switching to feature-rich, application-friendly alternatives, the company once had great success through broad attracting. Nokia works with around thirty-five hundred small companies, many of which sought Nokia, rather than vice versa. Through broad attracting, Nokia was able to get an option on nearly every new technology related to core GSM mobile phones (for more detail on Nokia's attracting activities, see sidebar 2-3). Nokia recently moved to a Windows operating system and introduced a new range of smartphones, so it remains to be seen whether Nokia can regain its capability to attract. But to benefit from attracting a stream of inbound knowledge, a company must possess the following specific qualities:

- *Respected brand and technology or industry leadership.* Knowledge holders aspire to getting their ideas or innovations adopted by companies that they and their peer group admire. Companies that represent the pinnacle of innovation in their industry are able to attract the best ideas. For example, in the auto industry, BMW meets this criterion and, as a result, attracts external knowledge for innovation. Similarly, Apple, which stands out for its technology and product innovation, is a beacon for innovative global technologies.

- *Leading market share.* Knowledge holders want their ideas to be widely implemented and, consequently, gravitate toward companies that have strong market share.

- *Good reputation for working with other companies.* A company that has a reputation for "hovering" its partners in order to gain a disproportionate advantage from new knowledge will find it difficult to attract others. Holders of new knowledge are likelier to approach companies known for being good, fair, and trustworthy partners.

SIDEBAR 2-3

NOKIA: ATTRACTING LEADING-EDGE RESEARCH

Nokia leveraged its strong brand and credibility as a leading innovator and as the market leader for mobile communication in order to boost its corporate research activities by attracting university research and entrepreneurial ideas worldwide. Nokia defines its broad innovation interests and posts them on the Internet. Recently for example, these included enterprise services, consumer and community services, human interface, content and search, and platform architectures, among others. Each area is then drilled down into more specific areas of research interest. Researchers from anywhere in the world can contact Nokia to discuss the relevance of their own research and propose a research project within one of the specified domains.

From Nokia's perspective, this approach to sensing and innovation meant it could cast a wide net and tap into research that it wouldn't otherwise have known about. The researchers who approach Nokia with their ideas wanted their innovations to be commercialized by an industry leader and to work with Nokia's own researchers.

Nokia's research leaders are responsible for vetting the inflow of ideas and selecting the proposals to carry forward. Depending on the nature of the proposed research, Nokia might enter into a confidential contract with an external researcher (when the innovation has the potential to provide unique value to Nokia) or embark on an open innovation project (if the research is likely to benefit the wider mobile telecoms ecosystem more generally). Alternatively, Nokia might introduce the idea to one of its ecosystem partners if it knew the research was a direct fit with their interests.

In a departure from the usual contract research model, Nokia involves its own researchers in the projects proposed by external parties. Depending on the nature of the project and, in particular, how explicit or tacit the knowledge created is likely to be, Nokia often colocates a team of its researchers to work with the university scientists in their labs. This allows the smooth integration of the innovation into Nokia's pipeline. So while it uses an attracting approach for identifying new knowledge, its choice between approaches for accessing is contingent on the nature of the knowledge it seeks.

When companies want to cut the cost of their innovation footprint and have the requisite qualities to engage in broad attracting, this mode of access may seem an appealing alternative to costly sites. But they should proceed with caution. The type of knowledge that a company can access by attracting is limited to complementary and codified knowledge, even when its creation has been sponsored through focused attracting. Its characteristics mean that it is more quickly replicable by competitors than embedded technological or complex and locally rooted knowledge. Attracting is only suitable when the knowledge the company is seeking has the following characteristics:

- *Explicit.* Technical or scientific knowledge codified in blueprints, drawings, code, manuals, and prototypes that can travel independently of the environment in which it was created and can be understood without reference to its originating context.

- *Owned.* Someone or some entity has to own or hold the knowledge that can be attracted, indicating a bias for knowledge with strong intellectual property rights.

- *Close or complementary to existing core knowledge base.* The type of knowledge that can be attracted is most likely to be used as part of a subsystem or system within products or services and, as such, needs to be close to a company's existing knowledge base.

An Agile and Balanced Optimized Footprint

We began this chapter warning of the dangers of overdependence on bricks-and-mortar innovation networks; they are expensive to set up and run, inflexible, inefficient and are based on historical knowledge requirements not current and emerging ones. But at the other end of the spectrum are companies that for reasons of organic growth or fear of losing the benefits of colocated innovation depend too heavily on virtual networks to access ever-increasingly dispersed knowledge. Though not as costly or inflexible as physical footprints, an overreliance on virtual networks is equally damaging: the type of knowledge that can be accessed is limited to the explicit variety—knowledge that competitors can easily copy. Virtual innovation networks don't provide access to the richness of embedded or complex knowledge. A virtual network is analogous to fishing in a trout stream. It's perfect if you want to catch only trout. But if you want variety, then you will have to trawl the oceans, too.

The key to achieving an innovation footprint that delivers agility and flexibility and is able to cast its net wide as well as deep is to adopt a balanced approach that involves experiencing, foraying, and attracting. These three different approaches are not mutually exclusive but should be constituent elements in delivering an effective and efficient global innovation strategy.

It is highly unlikely that any company can build an agile innovation network by focusing exclusively on one of the approaches we outlined, as this would imply that the company needs access to only one type of knowledge, simple and codified or context-dependent. Different parts of the innovation process rely on different types of knowledge. In a colocated environment, there is no similarity in finding a solution for a specific problem related to the development of an individual component and in trying to develop an entirely new product family to meet emerging customer requirements; the former requires technical precision and problem solving, while the latter needs an understanding of what those latent needs are and the creative solutions to meet them. As table 2-1 summarizes, this same logic should extend to thinking about an innovation network. The nature of the knowledge the company is seeking, the relative position of the company, and the characteristics of the knowledge source all play a role in defining which approach—experiencing, foraying, or attracting—a company should adopt. By aligning an innovation approach to the nature of the knowledge needed, a company can transform a hodgepodge of disparate global sites into a strategic function that delivers value, efficiency, and effectiveness through a flexible, focused, and dynamic innovation process.

Given that the trends of increasing knowledge dispersion and diversity are more likely to intensify than dissipate, having an optimized global innovation footprint is a critical factor in the innovation strategies of successful companies. While much

TABLE 2-1

Approaches to accessing new knowledge

	Attracting	Foraying	Experiencing
Characteristics of the knowledge	• Explicit • Complementary to core knowledge base • Codified • Owned • Modular	• Embedded • Close to core knowledge base • Observable • Replicable • Loosely definable	• Complex • Locally rooted • Difficult to define • Tacit and systemic • Context-dependent
Features of the recipient organization	• Respected leading brand • Image of technology leadership • Good reputation for alliances, partnering • Knowledge architecture must be clear and well defined	• Suitable for any organization Subject to availability and selection of suitable scouts	• Applicable to any organization willing to make significant resource and management commitments
Features of the knowledge source	• Global and broad range of knowledge sources (smaller companies, research institutes)	• Identifiable knowledge holders in specific locations	• Diffuse ownership
Implementation initiatives	• Locus of innovation firmly in home market • Combine and complement	• Locus of innovation in home market • Scouts to find, access, and relay knowledge • Lightweight and flexible • Learn and replicate	• Establish a local presence • Learn by doing and being there • Learn, combine, and complement

of the agility and flexibility in that footprint will be delivered through foraying and attracting activities, companies still need to make costly investments in sites. In the next chapter, we examine how to make the most judicious decisions about getting value from long-term sites in terms of their roles and the optimal size of a physical network.

CHAPTER THREE

How a Site Creates Value and Why the Size of the Network Matters

K nowing when foraying and attracting are better alternatives to a physical site isn't in itself enough to create an efficient, effective innovation network. In a truly optimized innovation footprint, a company establishes individual sites and organizes them with value creation at their core. Each must serve a specific purpose and contribute value in a clearly defined way. Intuitively, most managers understand that they can make significant gains from optimizing the configuration of their innovation networks. Our survey on global innovation revealed that managers believed that they could dramatically enhance both the speed and quantity of innovations by better configuration of their physical innovation footprints. But it seems that defining the optimal configuration is not something most companies have thought about systematically.

Ironically, while increased knowledge dispersion opens a myriad of new opportunities for companies to enhance their innovation capabilities, it also increases the potential for failure: when there is less certainty about where to place bets, companies face the dual risks of omission and commission. The risk of omission is the failure to include a site that should be part of an innovation network. Not opening in a new location could spell disaster if that location proves to be critical to innovation in an industry by becoming a center of technology invention, an important new competency base, a lead location for a new business model, or the home of leading-edge consumer demand. The risk of commission is the flip side and relates to the inclusion of sites that don't contribute value to an innovation network. These are legacy sites acquired through acquisitions, established by past strategies to be close to production, or located in a company's home country.

To manage the risks of omission and commission, companies need to assess the likely value of any given current or potential new bricks-and-mortar site in their network. Whether faced with the challenge of optimizing an existing innovation footprint, or in the early stages of building a global innovation network, firms need to ask the same questions and apply the same principles in assessing the contribution of a site. They should decide on the desirability of every site according to whether that site can contribute value based on the nature of innovation in any given industry.

In the first half of this chapter, we propose a framework for thinking about individual sites in terms of achieving one of three distinct, although not mutually exclusive, types of value. The first level, *substitution*, focuses on lowering costs through increased quality and productivity. The second, *complementarity*, aims to harness diverse and differentiated knowledge for innovation, while the final level, *discovery*, seeks new opportunities for more radical or game-changing innovations. We also highlight the dynamic nature of the network—a challenge presented by organizing innovation sites around this value-creation logic. Over time, the role of sites can change, for example, as new competences develop and current ones become redundant, the leading sources of critical customer knowledge shift, or the innovation regime in an industry changes (witness the move to digital photography and mobile communications). As a result, some sites will naturally evolve from functioning in one value dimension to another; others will no longer have a role to play and the company may need to establish new sites.

After looking at the value-creation dilemma at the level of the individual site, we then address the issue of ensuring that the whole bricks-and-mortar innovation footprint is also creating value. This means understanding how many sites in a network will ensure that the costs of managing and running that network (the integration and coordination costs) don't exceed the value being created. We describe some knowledge- and company-specific determinants that affect and define how dispersed or not a firm should be in order to balance cost and value.

Innovation Footprints: A Value-Based Approach

Value has become a ubiquitous term, not only in the management lexicon, but in a wider set of contexts, but there is little consensus about what it actually means. We asked a group of senior R&D managers from sixteen companies (and eight different countries) how they would define whether an individual site in their innovation network was creating or adding value. There were almost as many different answers as people: for some, it was about the number of patents per site; for others, delivering new products or services on time and on budget. Some mentioned metrics, including productivity and defects per site, as well as the relative cost of conducting R&D at different sites. What is perhaps most striking about these answers isn't the lack of consensus but the fact that without exception, and without being prompted, everyone in the group gave ex-post performance measurements of "value." While this type of appraisal can play a role in deciding whether to close or pare down existing sites, it isn't in the least helpful in judging the potential value a new site can bring.

To build an optimized global innovation footprint that will deliver sustained competitive advantage actually requires an ex-ante, systematic way of thinking about how individual sites can or should create value. As the value diamond in figure 3-1 illustrates, there are three distinctive dimensions on which individual sites can create value in an innovation network:

- *Substitution.* Substitution sites are about creating value by "doing what we already do but cheaper." This doesn't automatically equate with an arbitrage logic of chasing ever-lower costs by heading to the next low-wage country. Instead, substitution sites excel through greatly increased productivity per unit of innovation or R&D expenditure.

- *Complementarity.* It can be helpful to think of innovation as a jigsaw puzzle with complementarity value created by sites contributing pieces in the form of knowledge and expertise. An effective and efficient dispersed network doesn't have big overlaps or gaping holes. Because some of the knowledge needed for innovation is increasingly found outside a company's internal boundaries, complementarity sites also need to tap the wider local innovation ecosystem.

- *Discovery.* In discovery sites, the purpose is to find new opportunities by looking at the world differently, looking for different things, and then building new value-creating knowledge links. Creating value at this level means being in locations that may yield interesting new knowledge. Discovery activities involve experimenting with new approaches, ideas, and knowledge combinations and coexperimentation with new partners. This results in products, services, and solutions that are more likely to be radical innovations that competitors will find difficult to copy.

FIGURE 3-1

The value diamond

An innovation footprint delivering value at three levels

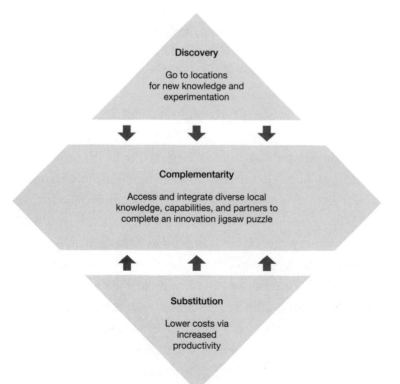

The optimal proportions of the value diamond changes for different companies, given that the nature of innovation differs across industries, companies within an industry have different competitive strategies and positions, and the state of their innovation pipelines vary dramatically. For firms that undertake a high level of routine R&D work, such as clinical trials in the traditional chemistry-based pharmaceutical industry, the complementarity dimension contracts, while the need for substitution sites increases. Companies in industries that deliver a constant stream of new products or services with short cycle times are more likely to focus on the complementarity sites needed to access the dispersed knowledge to fuel their innovation pipeline.

The following sections describe the roles of substitution, complementarity, and discovery sites; how to recognize where to best locate these sites; the potential pitfalls of setting up and managing each type of site; and the dynamic issues that can arise within this value-creating dispersed network.

Creating Substitution Value

The rationale for substitution activities is to "to do what we already do, but at lower cost." On the face of it, this argument would seem to have struck a chord with many companies over the past decade or so. The allure of reducing the cost of R&D and customer support, for example, has been high on company agendas, as witnessed by the rapid growth of the low-wage sites companies have established not only in India and China, but in Eastern Europe and South America. But this pursuit of low-wage innovation isn't the way to achieve substitution value. Today it may seem effective, but it is sure to destroy value tomorrow. Always chasing the next low-wage location carries with it significant setup and transaction costs that can quickly outweigh any benefits.

Reaping Potential Productivity Gains

Lowering costs isn't about paying people less, particularly when wage inflation will quickly eliminate those gains. Creating value at the substitution level is about taking a long-term perspective and finding sustainable solutions for reducing the cost of innovation. This can only be achieved by leveraging local capabilities and conditions to create centers of excellence that will deliver inherently high productivity gains long after wage differentials have been eradicated. Many companies in the pharmaceutical sector are doing exactly this by moving clinical trials to Singapore. Wages in the city state are only slightly lower than in many Western countries, but the costs of conducting clinical trials are significantly lower, thanks to higher productivity fueled by favorable regulations, excellent hospitals, and a world-class scientific research infrastructure.

When planning a substitution center of excellence in a new location, staffing issues are key. First, a sufficiently large talent pool is needed to meet the demands of an influx of multinationals and local players without driving both wage costs and staff turnover rates to unsustainable levels. Second, the offer of a long-term career playing a critical role in a global innovation network is more likely to attract high-caliber recruits than offering basic low-grade work based on crude arbitrage logic.

The human resource challenge becomes greater over time because keeping talented employees means offering them career development paths and, as they gain experience, more challenging and creative work (see chapter 1). This naturally leads to increased churn rates as companies need to recruit new employees to replace those moving to new roles, a cycle that makes sustaining a pure substitution site difficult. If the site has the potential to make a differentiated contribution to innovation, the company can add complementarity activities to the original substitution role of that site. For example, GE's John F. Welch Technology Center (JFWTC) in Bangalore, India, was established as a substitution site at the beginning of the millennium (see sidebar 3-1). With just three hundred employees, it was the group's center of excellence for computational analytics. It has excelled in this substitution role, with around 80 percent of analytical work across all of GE's global businesses currently taking place at JFWTC. Over the past decade, it has also become a complementarity site and, by 2012, was GE's largest multidisciplinary integrated innovation hub, employing over four thousand.

SIDEBAR 3-1

JOHN F. WELCH TECHNOLOGY CENTER: FROM SUBSTITUTION TO COMPLEMENTARITY IN INDIA

When GE opened the John F. Welch Technology Center (JFWTC) in 2000, it wasn't a newcomer to conducting research in India. GE Plastics had a long-standing and successful research agreement with the National Chemistry Lab in Poona, which provided the group with not only a perspective on Indian technologies relating to plastics but a gauge of the quality of intellectual capital available in India. So when GE Plastics proposed opening its own lab in India, then-CEO Jack Welch responded by suggesting that a new Indian lab should encompass all of GE.

To integrate the JFWTC, GE recruited around 30 percent of the site's staff from its existing innovation centers around the world; many were overseas Indians. They not only legitimized the new site and brought much needed knowledge to hasten the site's ability to create value, but also provided critical links between JFWTC and the existing organization by being sensitive to both contexts.

Senior managers also played a critical role in integrating the site by explicitly communicating their commitment and enthusiasm for the new center and outlining its phased growth plan. The center started small and focused on advanced data-analysis substitution activities deliverable across all of GE's businesses. Importantly, this didn't cost jobs elsewhere in the organization because the computer simulation processes carried out at JFWTC called for new and different competencies.

Over the following decade as JFWTC grew (reaching twenty-five hundred employees by early 2008 and over four thousand by 2011), GE entered into new areas based on the local competencies and knowledge it could access. For example, GE's energy group was able to reduce the noise created from wind turbines thanks to work done at JFWTC. The Indian center also made a significant contribution to the GE90 jet engine by designing high-strength, lightweight fan blades that help reduce fuel consumption by around 20 percent. JFWTC's contribution to complementarity was such that it is responsible for around half of GE's total global research patent activity.

In addition to leveraging its capabilities to contribute to global innovation projects, JFWTC has been at the forefront of entering new markets. Thanks to innovations born at JFWTC, GE Healthcare has developed a whole range of innovative, low-cost medical devices, including a handheld ultrasound device, a high-frequency X-ray machine, and portable electrocardiograms (ECGs).

(*continued*)

ECG machines common in the West cost around $10,000 and require specialist doctors to interpret their results. GE Healthcare recognized an opportunity to provide ECGs at much lower cost in India. The team at JFWTC developed a lightweight, portable ECG, the MAC 400. It is powered by rechargeable batteries and can perform one hundred ECGs per charge. It is simple to operate, and software interprets the data and prints out a report. At a cost of only $1,000, it is significantly cheaper than standard ECG machines and yet uses the same algorithm employed in all of GE's ECG devices.[1]

Integrating New Substitution Sites

In the realms of innovation and, more particularly, R&D, employees in developed markets often see the establishment of low-cost centers in emerging economies as a direct threat to their livelihoods. Our conversations with executives and technical personnel at many new substitution innovation centers in emerging economies revealed that it wasn't unusual to find the employees at new sites being set up to fail: They were not involved in the pre-project process. They were frequently sent incomplete or incorrect specifications that made it impossible for them to successfully perform their work. They were rarely provided with knowledge about previous or existing product families. And they weren't given access to people from other functions involved in the project, making it impossible for them to understand issues of interoperability, design, customer requirements, and interfaces. Once the project was underway, they were cut out of communication loops. Without representation at project meetings, personal networks, a senior management champion, or historical credibility, they struggled to make their voices heard. Even if a low-cost innovation center has leading-edge capabilities to offer, under these circumstances it's impossible to capture substitution value.

Integrating substitution activities is crucial to deriving value. At one level, this means implementing harmonized processes and providing full access to technical and knowledge repositories. On a more challenging level, it means communicating the site's role and purpose to the wider innovation organization in order to gain its acceptance. The most effective way of achieving this is by creating a high degree of connectivity among employees during the early years of the site's establishment.

Schneider Electric's substitution innovation site in Shanghai provides a good example of the level of connectivity required to integrate a new site. First, there are several senior expatriate managers, not only from the home base in France but also from other sites in the global network. There are a handful of midlevel expats who are involved in project teams. In addition, there are some junior expats who are part of Schneider's "Marco Polo" program, which sends talented young people to work in different countries for two years. And finally, there is a constant stream of visitors from other innovation sites who are working on dispersed projects that involve the Shanghai site. But this traffic isn't just one way. A number of Chinese Marco Polo staff are working in other Schneider innovation centers around the world. This may seem like an expensive and heavyweight approach. However, Schneider's Shanghai innovation center is well integrated into global project work, and its contribution adds significant value and reduces costs.

If It's Only About Arbitrage, Then Think Again

Choosing a location based on arbitrage logic is a dangerous strategy because the benefits are overstated and short-lived. Arbitrage sites suffer from high attrition rates due to the lack of career prospects for local staff. This prevents the sites from building a valuable body of knowledge locally and, in a vicious cycle, will reinforce the idea that the low-cost center is only capable of low-grade and repetitive work. As wages inevitably rise, along with management and coordination costs, this low-cost work will begin to look very expensive.

Yet, we acknowledge that basic work such as testing, verification, drafting, and so forth needs to be done. For companies seeking short-term low-cost development in the more basic innovation functions, the solution may be to outsource it to specialist third parties such as Wipro and Infosys. By specializing in specific activities, and offering training and strong career paths to young graduates in which they can become team and project managers or client liaison managers, these types of companies have found a way to run a sustainable (and profitable) operation performing what may seem to be the more mundane aspects of innovation.

Creating Value from Complementarity

To misquote the Renaissance poet John Donne, "No innovation center is an island entire of itself, each one is a piece of the continent, a part of the main."[2] In essence, this provides a good description of the complementarity element of an innovation network, with each site creating value via the unique and individual contribution it makes to the whole. Complementarity is about tapping differentiated contributions in the form of market insights, well-honed capabilities, or strong relationships with key external parties and bringing them together to build competitive advantage.

Novartis provides a good example of a company that has deliberately built an innovation footprint to achieve complementarity and leverage diversity and dispersion without duplication or redundancy. For example, the headquarters of the Novartis Institutes for Biomedical Research is in Cambridge, Massachusetts, near leading academic research centers and research hospitals. There is a major hub in Basel, Switzerland, a traditional center of excellence for drug discovery. A specialist center in Singapore focuses on tropical diseases, and another in China concentrates on infectious diseases like hepatitis (China has around a third of the world's hepatitis-infected population), while a lab in La Jolla, California, specializes in genomics. Each node in the network accesses knowledge specific to its location and, through collaboration, makes a differentiated contribution to the group's global innovation effort. In the three years prior to 2011, this complementarity approach helped Novartis gain more approvals for new molecular entities in both the United States and Europe than its competitors.

Building or reconfiguring an innovation network to derive value from complementarity involves mapping the jigsaw puzzle to build a picture of the knowledge required for innovation and its location. Figure 3-2 shows a simple tool to use for the mapping process. By assigning all the knowledge elements needed for innovation to spokes on the chart, plotting the degree to which those capabilities and knowledge are available at each site along the spoke, and then charting the knowledge map for each site, a picture of the location of knowledge, the overlaps and duplication, and the knowledge gaps develops. The map in figure 3-2 shows that in spite of having innovation sites in five different locations, the company isn't currently able to access the knowledge it needs in area D. Furthermore, although it has good access to knowledge elements A, B, G, and H, there is a degree of duplication for knowledge G, as both locations one and four access the same type of knowledge. The overlap in knowledge access at the center of the spokes is essential

FIGURE 3-2

Creating knowledge maps and identifying knowledge gaps

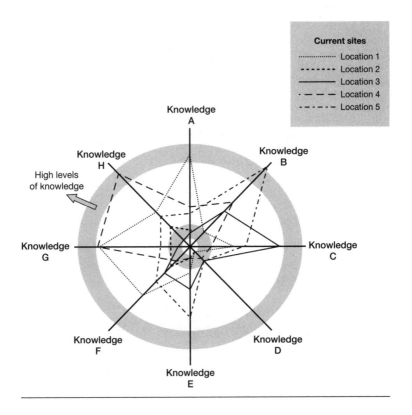

for enabling sites to integrate diverse knowledge from other locations. Mapping the jigsaw puzzle isn't a one-off activity. The rapid dispersion and diversification of knowledge needed for innovation means that a company should undertake the mapping regularly.

Only when a company has built a knowledge map can it understand where it needs to locate innovation centers and what roles they each need to play. Prior to the reorganization of its innovation activities, Novartis had its main U.S. innovation center in New Jersey, but when it identified biomedical research as critical to its innovation needs, it found this competency in the academic research cluster in Cambridge, Massachusetts. Novartis established a new innovation hub there to access world-class talent, tap leading-edge research from neighboring MIT, and collaborate with the Massachusetts General Hospital and other Boston-area research hospitals and local biotech companies.

Complementarity Requires Collaboration

Achieving value through complementarity necessitates that structures, processes, and incentives be established to allow the network to function as an integrated whole. Many innovation centers have for too long operated as mini-fiefdoms or walled cities, building an impressive array of capabilities to support their own activities yet not establishing appropriate linkages with other centers. As we will discuss in chapter 6, levels of collaboration across innovation networks are often woefully inadequate. Yet collaboration is a prerequisite to gaining complementarity value.

The greater the complementarity between sites and the fuller the cospecialization, the better the built-in incentive for collaboration. But there must be common systems and processes across sites, mechanisms and tools to support knowledge sharing (see chapter 5), a culture of openness, and appraisal methodologies that reward collaboration. Senior managers need to send clear messages about the roles each site is playing so that employees feel secure and therefore more willing to collaborate. Without these processes and incentives, the collaboration vital to gain complementarity value will be difficult, if not impossible, to attain.

Extending Beyond Internal Boundaries

Even with a well-designed innovation footprint, it's unlikely that any company will have access internally to the full complement of knowledge required for innovation. Gaining complementarity value relies on the building of not only quality internal resources but also collaborative relationships with external sources of knowledge. Our innovation survey revealed that companies tend to form partnerships and alliances in places where they already have a physical presence. This makes sense, because managing alliances can be an intensive and complex process that is aided by physical proximity. It could therefore be possible that the complementarity value of a site is through accessing and integrating diverse knowledge from partners, customers, suppliers, research institutes, local entrepreneurial companies, or R&D consortia.

Discovery Value: A World of Potential

Most companies find that creating value at the top of the diamond in figure 3-1, at the discovery level, is perhaps the most difficult. Discovery activities force companies to face unfamiliar and challenging scenarios that require them to examine new questions and perspectives. Sometimes these are found in what we call harbinger environments, places that are the forerunners of change of one kind or another. Sometimes, accelerated learning environments hold the key to discovery value by allowing rapid cycle experimentation, while in some instances, local regulatory environments force development of new, alternative approaches.

Harbingers

That companies in Finland and Sweden played such a leading role in breakthrough mobile telecom innovation is no coincidence. That India rather than one of the world's developed markets was the site for GE's development of a very low-cost portable ECG machine or that Japan has been home to so many radical portable electronic innovations from the Walkman and DS gaming console to i-mode is also not a coincidence. Long before any of these locations became well known for these innovations, all could be identified as harbingers for change.

Harbinger locations have one or more of the following distinguishing features:

- *Social phenomenon.* Certain societies or groups within societies exhibit distinct behavior and needs that call for very different product or service solutions. For example, an unusually high number of single-occupancy households and households with both adults employed full-time, combined with long working hours and the high cost of eating in restaurants, makes the United Kingdom the forerunner for innovation in high-quality ready-made meals. China, with its large number of young people born under its single-child policy, offers the potential for innovative Web-based social networking services.[3]

- *Demographics.* Large, aging, young, or newly wealthy populations all offer the potential to discover different unmet needs. So, for example, there would be no better place to go than Japan or Finland (where the population is aging most rapidly) to uncover opportunities for new products and remote services aimed at the elderly.

India, China, and Brazil provide insights into what is needed at the bottom of the pyramid.[4]

- *Physically determined.* The geography or topography of a location can have a big impact on what products and services a company develops. For example, Scandinavian and Nordic countries have small populations spread over a vast and often difficult terrain. The need to overcome geographic hurdles resulted in the early adoption of mobile radio phones in the 1920s; more recently, the region has become a leading location for remote health-care and diagnostic services.

Harbinger locations give companies the opportunity to access emerging technical or market knowledge that can help shape their long-term innovation pipeline. But perhaps of even greater value is the opportunity these locations provide for taking advantage of their unique facets to experiment with new business models. When Novartis established its Institute for Tropical Diseases (NITD) in Singapore, it recognized a harbinger location from which it could learn about and experiment with low-cost drug-delivery models (see sidebar 3-2). A confluence of social phenomenon, demographics, and physical determination meant that Singapore offered unique opportunities for Novartis.

SIDEBAR 3-2

NOVARTIS INSTITUTE FOR TROPICAL DISEASES: LEARNING FROM A NEW LOCATION

With the dominant business model in the pharmaceutical sector under threat, then-CEO Daniel Vasella and Paul Herrling, director

---

of corporate R&D, saw an opportunity to enter an emerging field in a different location and experiment with a new business model. They established the Novartis Institute for Tropical Diseases (NITD) to discover treatments and prevention methods for major tropical diseases that would be made available free to the developing world, while royalties from sales of the drugs in the developed world would flow back into the institute to fund continued research.

The nature of drug development was a deciding factor in NITD's location: it had to be in an area where tropical diseases were prevalent in order to have access to infected tissue samples. For this purpose, Africa, South America, or Asia would all have been suitable. However, one of the fundamental tenets of NITD was that it should act as a magnet for collaboration among entities interested in tropical diseases. Looking at the potential locations through this lens meant Novartis needed to find a region where it could have access to strong local partners with deep expertise. In addition, it needed to hire a relatively large pool of local scientists. To meet these requirements, Asia stood out as the best location.

Vasella and Herrling chose Singapore as the base for NITD. Singapore had received huge investments in life sciences, and many of the new companies that had been established were doing work that was very complementary to NITD, including the Genomics Institute of Singapore (which was responsible for sequencing the SARS virus) and the Bioinformatics Institute of Singapore. NITD required a large pool of local scientists from which to recruit and also needed to attract world-class scientists. Singapore scored well on both fronts: despite its small population, it had many science graduates, and its excellent housing, schooling, health care, and leisure facilities made it an attractive option for expatriates.

After years of guarded secrecy about its science, with NITD, Novartis was experimenting with a new business model that
(continued)

relied on collaboration with scientific institutes, universities, other pharmaceutical companies, and nongovernmental organizations (NGOs). The NGOs, which have generally been fierce critics of the pharmaceutical industry, were key to NITD. NGOs such as Médecins Sans Frontières (MSF), and the Red Cross with the World Health Organization (WHO) worked in the developing world, struggling daily to treat people with fatal diseases in poor conditions and without access to the arsenal of drugs in the pharmacies of most hospitals in the West. They knew more about the symptoms, progress, and treatment of tropical diseases than anyone else in the world. From the early planning days of NITD, Novartis involved NGOs in its discussions, so by the time NITD was up and running, those old enemies had become vital supporters and collaborators in its work.

Exploiting value from harbinger locations needn't require huge new investments. India and China, for example, offer an opportunity that few companies seem to have grasped. They provide a chance to experiment with new technologies, new markets, and new business models. Both have huge talent pools, unique social phenomena, face significant challenges, and are currently very cheap. It makes sense to give innovation centers in these locations a mandate to experiment.

Accelerated Learning Environments

In their 1993 book, *Art & Fear*, artists David Bayles and Ted Orland recount the following story.[5] A ceramics teacher divided a class in two and told one group of students that they would be graded on the quantity of work they produced over the term, while the other would be graded on the quality of a single piece of pottery. When grading the work, the teacher found that, without exception, all of the best-quality pieces were actually produced by the group focusing on quantity. These results had nothing to do with the relative skills of the students at the outset of the assignment. What had happened was that the students in the group focusing on quantity created so many pieces of work that they were learning from their mistakes and consequently improving with every piece they produced. The other group, working on perfecting one piece, didn't have the same opportunity to learn.

The same holds true for innovation. Rapid cycle, collective, and continual learning yields much better results than a more narrow focus. Take the example of wind turbines, which are complex machines involving electronics, mechanics, hydraulics, aerodynamics, and advanced materials. In the United States, companies were pitted against each other to create breakthrough technologies that would give them a leading edge over their competitors in what they saw as a potentially lucrative field. In Denmark, a different model of innovation developed. The Danes took a collaborative approach based on experimentation and incremental problem solving: the companies and suppliers involved created a learning network that also included the national testing body and government regulators. Just like the quantity potters, the Danish industry continually learned from its mistakes and was able to adapt and improve its products rapidly. The result was that the U.S. players significantly lagged behind their Danish counterparts; Denmark is now the world's leading center for wind turbine technologies, with a global market share of around 20 percent in 2011.

Leading or Lenient Regulatory Environments

The regulatory regime of any particular location can have a significant impact on the promotion of innovation and the development of local knowledge underlying it. When regulations limit or curtail the use of current technologies, hot spots for alternative or radical approaches can develop. California's zero-emission vehicle (ZEV) policy provides a good example. In 1990, the state introduced the ZEV regulation to encourage the development and commercialization of zero-emission vehicles. It stipulated that by 2003, 10 percent of new cars sold in the state would have to be ZEVs, rising incrementally thereafter. Although auto manufacturers have continually complained about this regulation and sought legal redress to overturn it, ZEV has in fact singled out California as a hub for innovation relating to lower-polluting technologies, including new fuel cells, electric vehicles, and also more environmentally friendly combustion engines. By 2010, ZEV requirements in California were exceeded, with over 2 million zero-emission vehicles registered.

Avoiding the Ivory Tower

Because they are more likely to focus on future-oriented innovation, discovery activities may be viewed as separate from other innovation work and risk falling under the radar completely. The tradition in some industries of allowing future-oriented, discovery-type research to exist in an ivory tower is not a recipe for value creation. In the same way that some substitution sites evolve to become complementarity sites, discovery sites that yield knowledge leading to successful innovations morph into complementarity sites. For a smooth transition to take place, it is vital that when this happens, discovery sites are already integrated into a company's global innovation network.

A summary of how to create value from sites

	Substitution	Complementarity	Discovery
Selecting site locations	• Local conditions help deliver significant productivity gains (i.e., skills, regulations, ecosystem) • Large local talent pool	• Identifying the knowledge required for innovation and mapping where it is located will reveal the most important locations for sites	• Harbinger locations; forerunners of change • Accelerated learning environments for rapid cycle experimentation • Regulatory regimes that force alternative approaches
What to do	• Sites should be centers of excellence • Well integrated into the global innovation network via processes, systems, connectivity, and access to technical and knowledge banks • Career structures in place to retain good staff	• Collaboration across sites is a prerequisite, with each site contributing unique knowledge • Use network to tap wider ecosystem as there is value from links with external players • Strong senior management support driving collaboration	• Access unfamiliar and new knowledge for architectural or radical innovation and to create new markets • Experiment with new business models, services, and technologies • Strong communication with business to share learning
Benefits	• Lower costs and higher quality • Faster cycle times and time to market	• Innovations created from a greater diversity of knowledge and capabilities (market insights, technologies, etc.)	• Supports the exploration of new opportunities to contribute knowledge for innovation
Potential pitfalls	• Don't confuse "low cost" with "low wage"; it's not arbitrage • Mundane and repetitive work doesn't add value and could be outsourced more effectively	• Lack of differentiation; redundancy and duplication across sites • Sites working as mini-fiefdoms will not contribute	• Difficult to measure value being created, risk of losing patience • If isolated from the business, potential innovations will be lost
Dynamics and evolution	• Over time, may evolve to become complementarity sites • May have to be downsized or closed	• Knowledge requirements need to be mapped regularly, which may result in site location changes	• Over time, sites that contribute knowledge for innovation will become complementarity sites

Buried Treasure: The Potential in Existing Subsidiaries

Many companies overlook their overseas operational subsidiaries as potential contributors to global innovation because historically they were either established as a quid pro quo with host governments for market access or acquired as the baggage of mergers or acquisitions. These subsidiaries are largely engaged in local adaptation. Even in a transnational model, local subsidiaries don't contribute knowledge to global innovation because each operates as a home base focusing on its own market.

Yet some local operational subsidiaries have forged a role for themselves as contributors to global innovation, which should prompt companies to look seriously at the potential buried in their own organizations. HP Singapore, for example, evolved from a low-cost manufacturing base to a key node in the group's innovation network involved in the development of ink-jet cartridges, networking products, and printers. Rather than being a home-base initiative, this transformation was pursued systematically over time by a local entrepreneurial executive constantly asking what unique contribution HP Singapore could make, based on its distinctive competencies. In terms of the value diamond in figure 3-1, by bringing unique skills and not just being a cheaper location, HP Singapore positioned itself to create complementarity value. Another example of how a subsidiary transformed itself from being a point for peripheral market access to a key global knowledge hub is the evolution of Fuji Xerox (see sidebar 3-3). There, as with HP Singapore, a determined, persistent, entrepreneurial local executive kept pushing for a more innovative role for Fuji Xerox.

SIDEBAR 3-3

FUJI XEROX: FROM MARKET ACCESS JOINT VENTURE TO KEY INNOVATION HUB

Fuji Xerox, a fifty-fifty joint venture between Xerox and Fuji Photo Film, was created in 1962 as a marketing, sales, and service entity to exploit Xerox's xerography patents in Japan. Tony Kobayashi, a Wharton School graduate and son of Fuji Photo Film's president, headed the new subsidiary.

By the late 1960s, it became increasingly obvious that Xerox's success in Japan was hampered by the size and complexity of its machines as well as its leasing and price-per-copy business model. New Japanese competitors, such as Canon and Ricoh, were developing and selling, rather than leasing, high-quality small copiers much more suitable to the requirements of the Japanese market. Seeing the writing on the wall, Kobayashi proposed that Xerox change its strategy in Japan, but the U.S. management decided to stick with its business model because it thought the margins from indirect sales on small machines would be too slim. So, to meet local demand for small copiers, Fuji Xerox went out on a limb, repackaging Xerox's technologies to develop a small and successful desktop copier.

Fortunately for Xerox, its reluctance to learn from the periphery was overcome when David Kearns was appointed vice president (later to become CEO) in 1971. Kearns had previously been at IBM, where he had seen what could be learned from Japan.

As competition intensified in the small-copier market outside Japan, Fuji Xerox developed a small copier for Rank Xerox,

(continued)

79

Xerox's joint venture in Europe. Around the same time, as its competence in quality management became apparent, it took control of manufacturing operations. By the late 1970s, when Xerox was forced by the U.S. government to relinquish exclusive control of its patents, Fuji Xerox was at the heart of the Xerox Group's response to Japanese global competition. Kobayashi was appointed to the board of the Xerox Group. Over the following years, whenever Xerox was in trouble over quality, product design, product policy, or its business model, it turned to Kobayashi for solutions he had piloted in Japan. In return, Kobayashi negotiated more innovation resources for Fuji Xerox and a wider sales territory.

In many senses, Fuji Xerox was better integrated into Xerox's innovation activities than were Xerox's businesses. It worked closely with the highly innovative Xerox PARC (Palo Alto Research Center), even colocating some of its research with PARC (while the Xerox group as a whole infamously overlooked many of the game-changing innovations developed there).

In the 1990s, the advent of digital printing and the increasing importance of computer networks further propelled Fuji Xerox into a more central role in Xerox's future. By the 2000s, as Xerox yet again found itself in a strategic crisis, Fuji Xerox stepped in and cemented its role as a center for the group's innovation.[6]

For companies that are building an optimized innovation network, it's obviously not feasible to wait and see if a confluence of the right people and circumstances leads to the transformation of an operational subsidiary into an innovation center. However, based on examples of transformation, it is clear that, when assessing the innovative potential of an operational subsidiary, certain enabling conditions need to be in place if the subsidiary is going to transform into a substitution, complementarity, or discovery value-creating node in the network:

- *Local learning environment.* The location should provide an opportunity for unique learning based on capabilities, customer requirements, or a local innovation ecosystem.

- *Local executive champion.* Either a local or an expatriate who is able to recognize the potential of the local environment and has the drive and wherewithal to exploit it. This executive also needs to have the skills and ability to build trust with other units and represent effectively the site's innovative potential. It is vital that he or she has the support of a good local management team able to sustain a strong voice in global deliberations.

- *Clear competence development path.* As a newcomer to the global innovation network, the subsidiary has to understand how it will develop and accumulate its capabilities. It must have something to offer beyond the short term.

- *Open and supportive corporate management.* For a subsidiary to contribute to global innovation, it requires globally focused corporate management. While this may sound obvious, the deeply rooted assumptions of home-country primacy in many firms actually make it difficult. The motto, "Think global, act local," needs to be turned on its head to "Think local, act global."

Balancing Cost and Value

Along with thinking about the value contributed by individual sites, companies also need to consider the big picture. How large should an innovation footprint be to ensure that the overall costs of increased complexity, management coordination, and communication don't outweigh the value it is creating?

The relentless march toward greater knowledge dispersion implies that having more sources of knowledge available substantially increases the potential for value creation. This logic can easily lead to the proliferation of sites in a global innovation network. But the marginal value of additional locations is likely to decline due to duplication and redundancy, while the marginal costs increase more than proportionately with each knowledge source added, as the costs of communication, coordination, collaboration, and integration grow. Knowing the number of sites required in an innovation network to avoid both commission and omission and achieve a balance between the cost of running the network and the value it creates isn't an exact science. Instead, a set of company- and knowledge-specific determinants define the optimal size of a footprint (see figure 3-3).

Intrinsic Dispersion of Knowledge Required for Innovation

The size of an innovation network depends in large part on the dispersion of the knowledge required. When most of the knowledge needed for innovation is on a company's doorstep, the dispersion of its innovation footprint reflects this. For example, many biotech firms didn't have to venture further than the San Francisco Bay area, home to a leading cluster of life science,

FIGURE 3-3

Predeterminants of footprint size and dispersion

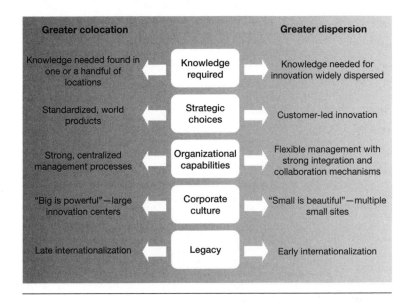

computer software, robotics, and microelectronics knowledge, all critical to the advancement of biotech.

Conversely, in some industries, relevant knowledge is highly dispersed. Take the example of liquid crystal displays (LCDs). While the underlying scientific breakthroughs of LCDs were largely European and American, they could not have been turned into commercially successful innovations without the process and learning skills of the Japanese semiconductor industry. If a single pixel is defective, the whole screen has to be scrapped, calling for extremely exacting standards of manufacturing quality. It's no coincidence therefore that all the successful early LCD innovations were the result of combinations of Western and Asian firms, such as IBM and Toshiba, Sharp and Corning, or Philips and LG, because a critical part of the knowledge needed for LCDs could only be found in Asia.

Strategic Choices Driving Footprint Size

Companies' strategic choices radically influence their innovation footprint and how far-flung it needs to be to maximize value. Compare the impact on footprint size and dispersion of the early strategic paths of two successful companies in the same sector, Intel and ST Micro. From its early years, Intel made a clear strategic choice to develop standardized products. It sold the same microprocessors to all customers around the world and achieved differentiation via how the microprocessors were then programmed for specific uses. For many years, this strategy enabled Intel to concentrate its innovation activities in its hometown of Santa Clara, California, and a couple of key centers in Oregon and Israel. As we will see in chapter 7, Intel's footprint subsequently expanded to incorporate collaborative labs with global partners, but even so, its strategy has enabled it to have very few innovation sites relative to the size of the company and still maintain innovation leadership.

In contrast, ST Micro, established in 1987 as the result of a merger of two failing state-owned semiconductor companies (from Milan and Paris), came late into the game. To differentiate itself, it adopted a strategy to develop application-specific "systems on a chip" (which became an enabling technology for the miniaturization of mobile phones and many other now ubiquitous electronic devices). To be successful, ST Micro needed an in-depth understanding of its customers' products and applications to build long-term relationships with them. This necessitated having a highly dispersed innovation footprint with centers located close to all its lead customers. In addition, it relied heavily on technology alliances to complement its limited home-base capabilities, and this further drove the need for dispersion. So, even within the same industry, the optimal size and dispersion of an innovation footprint depends to a great extent on the strategy a firm chooses.

Organizational Capability Constraints

A company needs very different capabilities to manage a highly dispersed innovation network than a colocated site. Firms that don't have the skills, processes, and mechanisms in place to manage dispersion therefore have a different optimal footprint configuration from those that do. Comparing Intel and ST Micro again, Intel had a centralized management culture with strong, systematic management processes that didn't leave room for local initiatives to emerge or flourish. Adding new R&D sites and dispersed design centers would have challenged Intel's management skills and called for developing new organizational capabilities—a significant cost to a company that was already highly successful with its limited dispersion.

At ST Micro, on the other hand, a small Franco-Italian team of globe-trotting, entrepreneurial executives led a highly flexible organization that relied on local innovation supported by strong organizational integration capabilities and the ability to collaborate across distances. Because the culture, structures, and processes needed for managing dispersion were in place, it was much easier for ST Micro to establish new sites. Having the organizational capabilities to manage dispersion meant the value created from adding new sites was greater than the management and coordination costs of the enlarged network.

Corporate Culture and Preferences

A culture of "small is beautiful" or "big is powerful" runs through corporate DNA. It has a profound effect on the choice firms make between dispersed small innovation sites and more colocated large ones and has an impact on the optimal cost-value balance for individual firms. Entrepreneurial companies tend to favor a greater number of small, creative, autonomous sites. For instance, in a bid to retain its entrepreneurial energy as it grew from a start-up to a global firm, W. L. Gore, the maker of Gore-Tex, applied what it called an "amoeba organization" principle. It achieved growth through the proliferation of small sites, organized in clusters. This allowed W. L. Gore to benefit from the informality and creativity of small sites and at the same time achieve a critical mass of diverse competencies in any one location.

The Impact of History and Legacy

The ability to create value from a dispersed footprint can also be affected by how and when a company internationalized. General Motors (GM), for example, internationalized at a time of separate national car markets and high tariff barriers, leading it to acquire companies like Vauxhall in Britain and Opel in Germany. It later continued to grow via acquisitions with Saab in Sweden and Daewoo in Korea. Each of its acquisitions brought R&D centers with capabilities well tailored to the national brand and local market. Contrast this with Toyota, which didn't begin to internationalize until the early 1960s in an age of falling trade barriers. Although the group established manufacturing plants in Australasia, its focus on developing "world cars" meant that Toyota could keep innovation and R&D at home.

Different historical heritages have led to GM and Toyota to very different innovation footprints. But dispersion isn't necessarily better. A highly dispersed footprint that operates in a multidomestic mode, without close integration and collaborative abilities, for example, will generate greater costs than value. It's therefore important to be aware of legacy constraints when building an optimized innovation network.

Innovation Footprints and Value Creation

No one can accurately predict where the next wave of critical knowledge in any industry will come from. However, we can with great certainty predict that it will be diverse in nature and dispersed in provenance. How companies build and align their innovation footprints needs to alter to reflect these changes. Yet merely adding new locations to an innovation footprint in order to access a wide knowledge base does not guarantee added value, as each site brings additional coordination and integration costs. Getting the size of an innovation network right to ensure that the value created from dispersion is greater than the cost of managing the dispersed network is difficult, because there is no single correct answer. Every company is starting from a different point, with the dispersion of critical knowledge, past strategic choices, organizational capabilities, legacy, and corporate culture all playing a part in defining the optimal size of a network. Of course, over time, as the footprint is reconfigured around differentiation and value creation, these factors play a less important role in determining the optimal cost-value balance and therefore the size of the network.

Whatever the optimal size of the network, there is a need for more drastic realignments and a new focus on thinking about innovation footprints in terms of an evolving portfolio in which individual sites create value at one or more of the three levels of substitution, complementarity, or discovery:

- Managers need to shift their perspective on what low-cost innovation means—from short-lived arbitrage opportunities to sustainable substitution activities. This means lowering costs through increased productivity of the more routine elements of innovation.

- Achieving value through complementarity should become the organizing principle for configuring the bulk of innovation activities. This requires mapping the innovation jigsaw puzzle to ensure that there are no knowledge gaps and that each site makes a differentiated contribution based on the best competencies and knowledge, without duplication.

- Finally, as cycle times shrink and entire innovation regimes face their demise, innovation needs to create value through discovery activities designed to explore new opportunities.

Achieving a value-creating innovation footprint doesn't necessarily mean closing existing sites and opening new ones. In some instances, it means a company should reassess the potential of what it already has. Sites in emerging economies can become valuable locations for experimentation and discovery, for example, while often overlooked operational subsidiaries may have the capabilities, local links, and drive to become con-tributors to complementarity value.

Clearly, failing to think about innovation footprints in terms of value creation leaves companies exposed and vulnerable to their more focused and agile competitors. It's also important to recognize the dynamic nature of innovation footprints. On one level, as the location of critical knowledge changes, managers need to realign footprints to reflect this. On another level, managers should be cognizant of the fact that internal dynamics can change the value-creating role of existing sites over time.

In part III, we move from footprint optimization to the next critical step of integrating the global innovation network through optimizing communication and receptivity.

OPTIMIZING COMMUNICATION AND RECEPTIVITY

Integrating the Network

CHAPTER FOUR

The Barriers to Integration

I n the previous chapters, we focused on strategies, tools, and processes aimed to optimize a company's innovation footprint. But having an ability to access knowledge from around the world in the most efficient, effective manner is of limited value without the capabilities to integrate and leverage that knowledge across the organization (see chapter 1 and figure 1-2). Take, for example, Snecma, which we discussed in chapter 2. The distinctive science Snecma found in Russia would have remained there had it not created the mechanisms and processes to first absorb the new knowledge and then integrate it into its own innovation pipeline. Similarly, Novartis's Institute for Tropical Diseases, which we discussed in chapter 3, would have turned into a costly white elephant that delivered little value at great cost and given the group no advantage over its competitors had it not succeeded in combining the new knowledge it accessed from NGOs, patient groups, and local institutions in Singapore with the company's traditional drug development activities.

In both these examples, Snecma and Novartis were able to succeed because they had optimized their communication channels and their receptivity or capability to absorb new knowledge. However, many companies that have relied on a colocated model of innovation find that building the capabilities to leverage knowledge across a dispersed innovation footprint is a significant challenge, one that requires a cultural change to underpin new tools and processes for sharing knowledge and connecting people. In this chapter, as outlined in table 4-1, we examine each of the main barriers to optimizing communication and

TABLE 4-1

Barriers to optimizing communication and receptivity

Barriers	Characteristics
Lack of receptivity	• Control and internal competition
	• Projector mind-set
	• Not invented here
Inadequate connections	
ICT systems for codified knowledge	• Incompatible IT systems
	• Large database repositories
IT systems to connect knowledge holders	• Isolated experts
	• Reinventing the wheel
Networks connecting sites and teams	• Extreme localism with lack of interaction between sites
Multiple different contexts	• Organization structure
	• Functional languages and world views
	• Cultures and norms
	• National languages
Transferring and integrating complex knowledge	• Can be difficult to recognize
	• Inherently difficult to share as rooted in originating context

receptivity: inadequate connections and mechanisms to share codified knowledge and connect knowledge holders; multiple contexts creating communication barriers between different parts of the organization; an inherent difficulty in transferring and integrating complex knowledge; and organizational cultures that fail to promote reciprocity.

Barriers to Optimizing Communication

There are many common adages, such as "knowledge is power" and "knowledge is the glue that holds organizations together," that hint at an underlying acknowledgment of the importance of knowledge as a resource. It wouldn't be unreasonable, therefore, to assume that since knowledge is deemed important, most organizations have well-designed strategies enabling them to transfer and integrate knowledge from around the world. After all, a successful global innovation footprint is one that accesses dispersed and differentiated knowledge and brings it together in innovative ways. This ability to transfer and integrate knowledge from multiple sources is key to building competitive advantage.

But, while many organizations pay lip service to the importance of knowledge, in reality, they keep it imprisoned in individual locations, functions, or business units. It is only powerful in a very limited, local sphere, if it all. And instead of binding the organization, its confinement serves to perpetuate distance and difference. Many companies fail to leverage the potential value of the knowledge they have access to.

So what causes this contradiction between the perceived importance of knowledge as a value-creating resource and a seeming inability to exploit its potential? Companies find it difficult to transfer and integrate knowledge between different parts of the organization because they face multiple, wide-ranging, and systemic barriers to freeing it and optimizing communication: people and places are rarely connected beyond a few personal relationships; differing contexts between locations and functions are an impediment to communication and knowledge transfer; and companies don't understand the requirements for transferring and integrating complex, rooted knowledge.

When we conducted our survey on global innovation, we were not surprised to learn that most companies experienced difficulties in sharing complex knowledge across different sites. The fact that this type of knowledge is rooted in behavior, norms, values, interactions, and systemic relationships all specific to the local environment hints at some of the potential challenges in moving it. As we saw in chapter 2, to access this type of knowledge requires immersion in the local context—to learn through experiencing. The nature of the knowledge itself makes its transfer and integration difficult.

What was more surprising from the survey, however, was that two-thirds of companies also reported difficulties in transferring explicit, codified knowledge between different parts of their organizations. Intuitively, this doesn't make sense. When knowledge isn't embedded or rooted in a local context, it should be able to move more freely. There is no inherent difficulty stemming from the nature of this knowledge that impedes its transfer. This means other factors are at play, which can prevent companies from leveraging even highly codified knowledge.

Understanding what factors are barriers to a firm's ability to successfully transfer and integrate knowledge, from the most explicit and codified to the highly complex, is crucial to moving toward optimized communication. First, there are inadequate connection mechanisms between different parts of the network, ranging from shared data repositories and ways of capturing experiential learning to processes and tools to support global communication and collaboration. Second, there is a lack of communication between different contexts and functions within organizations. Next are the inherent difficulties of transferring and integrating complex knowledge. Communication will only be successful if receptivity is improved and there is a culture of collaboration, openness, and transparency throughout the firm.

Inadequate Connections

Knowledge doesn't move by itself. Its transfer from one location to another depends on people facilitating and driving that movement, whether in the form of direct communication between individuals and teams or via an intermediary such as specifications, a database, or a CAD drawing. If nodes in an innovation network (by this, we mean either the individual, team, or site) are denied the tools and processes to connect to each other, or given inadequate solutions, knowledge will remain imprisoned in its originating location. There are three basic areas in which inadequate connections between these nodes are common: technology-based systems for handling codified knowledge; technology-based systems to connect knowledge holders and recipients for their knowledge; and mechanisms to build networks and bonds between various nodes.

Failure to Transfer Codified Knowledge via IT Systems

One of the most obvious barriers to the transfer of codified knowledge is a lack of adequate technology-based tools to support such transfer between different parts of an organization. This barrier manifests itself in two different ways. First is a lack of common systems. Decisions made by devolved purchasing control or poor postmerger integration activities result in a legacy of incompatible IT systems and work tools across different locations or functions. This makes it nearly impossible to connect different nodes: if systems can't talk to each other, there is no conduit for transferring codified knowledge. Interoperability and connectivity call for common systems, but these are costly to implement and require coordination to maintain and manage.

Second is the ineffective utilization of databases. Following the knowledge management boom in the early 1990s, companies made huge investments in electronic repositories, ranging from client profile systems to technical databases. They intended the knowledge stored in these to be available as a common resource. But few companies use these databases for anything other than archiving codified knowledge. They tend to be static, because the scope and organization of the knowledge they hold was predefined at the time of their original development. They are usually obsolete because only a few select individuals can update them, and the process for communicating necessary updates is often cumbersome or lacking. They are monolithic, as they sit firmly within functions and businesses, are costly to maintain, and have little relevance to daily operations and, as such, fail to create value.

Failure to Connect Knowledge Holders and Recipients Using ICTs

Dispersed across most organizations is a rich seam of underutilized experiential knowledge that can be easily articulated and transferred. Within any company on any given day, a new problem arises for which there is no immediately obvious solution. But in all likelihood, this same problem or a similar one has already been solved elsewhere in the organization. Does it really make sense to spend time and resources reinventing the wheel without seeing if the required knowledge already exists at another site? Yet many firms fail to leverage their technology resources to create tools that connect knowledge holders and enable individuals to seek advice or help from the wider community of experts within the organization. Without this, companies can't exploit valuable experiential knowledge effectively.

Failure to Create Networks and Build Bonds

In too many organizations, even with the plethora of enabling ICTs available, communication between individuals outside their immediate spheres of daily activities is woefully poor. Individuals don't naturally gravitate to building relationships with people they perceive as different or distant from themselves. Different nationalities, functional specialties, languages, training, culture, and so on are barriers to connectivity and communication. They blind people to the opportunities in viewing problems and solutions through perspectives other than their own. Even though the end result may be poorer, most people prefer to work within the comfort zone of their local peer group than with teams and individuals in far-flung places. Yet, even when they are aware of the benefits of wider connectivity, few companies have instituted the tools and processes to encourage and support the transfer of embedded knowledge between individuals and teams.

Multiple Different Contexts

One of the common difficulties companies confront when trying to connect nodes is that multiple contexts act as barriers to communication. The very structure of an organization and its subsidiaries prevents knowledge transfer. Although matrix structures have helped unify organizational structures and reporting lines across different locations, there is still scope for local variances to reinforce contextual differences between sites. Differing cultures and norms can inhibit understanding, empathy, or trust, while different national languages present a more obvious barrier to communication. But more divisive are those language barriers that describe processes and that people use as shorthand to explain complex concepts and ideas and frame contexts within different functions.

The Danger of Allowing Functional Enclaves to Flourish

We hosted a conference at INSEAD on the challenges of global innovation. During a session about the barriers to running an integrated global innovation network, the discussion veered toward the usual suspects of distance and the problems of time differences, national languages, and differing cultural norms and behavior. One of the participants, a senior R&D manager from a large U.S. technology firm, stood up and said that in his experience, distance wasn't such a serious barrier. He explained that working with other software engineers, whether they were in the same building in California or based thousands of miles away in India, Europe, or China, made little difference. As software engineers, they shared a functional language that supported rich communication and knowledge sharing. On the other hand, he hadn't had much success working with people from other functions who sat in the same building. They shared proximity, a national language, and a social, cultural context, but were separated by the gulf of different functional languages. A general murmur of agreement rippled through the lecture hall.

People in different functions in the value chain have diverse and distinct ways of looking at problems and solutions. Each function has developed its own shorthand language for complex ideas specific to that function. A problem arises because people from different functions don't necessarily understand the bedrock of complex ideas from other functions let alone have the skills to decode the shorthand. As we will see in chapter 6, this isn't just an issue between different functional activities such as marketing and technology development, but exists between more closely related activities such as mechanical and electrical engineering.

Functional barriers can have a detrimental impact on a company's ability to innovate successfully. As the proponents of such processes as "design for six sigma" point out, between 70 and 80 percent of manufacturing defects are actually caused by design decisions.[1] Imagine what companies could achieve, what efficiencies they could gain, and what robust products and services they could create if different functions transferred and shared knowledge throughout the innovation process instead of reinforcing their own fiefdoms.

Transferring and Integrating Complex Knowledge

The challenges that companies face in accessing complex knowledge (described in chapter 2) are due to its rooted, systemic, and diffuse characteristics. These same characteristics create a barrier to the transfer and integration of complex knowledge. The first difficulty is that it's not always easy to recognize that knowledge is locally rooted. A good, although often recounted, example is the Walt Disney Company's establishment of Euro Disney, later renamed Disneyland Paris. In the United States, Disney had a winning formula, attracting thousands of customers from all over the world. But the knowledge that made Disney parks so successful was locally rooted in American social and cultural norms. Disney discovered that not all elements of the successful U.S. formula, when transferred to Europe and a largely

French workforce, worked so well in the Paris-based park. For example, the ban on alcohol didn't translate from the wholesome U.S. family orientation to the European context, where a glass of wine is an integral part of lunch. In the U.S. parks, all interactions with customer services were met with a smile that indicated concern and sincerity. European customers, however, found it irritating, condescending, and highly inappropriate when their complaints to customer service staff at Disneyland Paris were met with the same smile.[2]

Disney failed to understand how context-dependent or complex much of its knowledge was. When establishing Disneyland Paris, it did not alter manuals and operating procedures from the U.S. parks before shipping them to the new location. Few of the management team had been to Europe before. It's therefore hardly surprising that Disney underestimated the differences between the U.S. and European contexts. A year after the French park opened and a local management team with international experience was put in place, the initial problems were rectified, with the Disney values and traditions finally transcribed and translated to fit the new context.

Even when it is easy to recognize that knowledge is complex, companies face significant difficulties in transferring and absorbing that knowledge. Few really understand what mechanisms and processes they need. The usual tools in the armory for transferring knowledge, such as reports, prototypes, databases, temporary assignments, and fleeting site visits simply don't fit the bill. The successful transfer and integration of complex knowledge rely on having managers with multicultural experience and companies understanding that results won't be achieved overnight.

Yet, our survey on global innovation uncovered an interesting paradox: the majority of companies recognized that people with multicultural experience were better at interpreting, absorbing, and using new knowledge, particularly from very different places. However, few of these same companies were actively building a cadre of people to fulfill this role through career structures and rewards. The worrying implication is that a great many companies don't have people with the capabilities to share and integrate complex knowledge. Unless these companies take this challenge seriously, they will face increasing difficulty accessing and integrating the more complex and rooted dispersed knowledge that is key to remaining competitive.

Barriers to Optimizing Receptivity

Even if companies manage to overcome all the barriers to optimizing communication, they will still ultimately fail if they don't build a culture of contribution and exchange across their organization. Companies need to become more receptive, overturning a deep-seated cultural bias toward working with people who seem close geographically, culturally, and professionally. Becoming more receptive means challenging beliefs, assumptions, and behavior not only at the level of organizational culture, but also at the level of how individual employees define innovation, because the idea that "knowledge is power" thrives at the individual and team levels, with a premium on original creation and few incentives to encourage knowledge sharing.

Traditionally, organizations that were successful in conquering the world did so by tightly controlling costs, ideas, personnel, and behavior and focusing on competition both with external players and internally between different divisions. When innovation was a more local affair and the knowledge needed to deliver successful innovations was less dispersed and diverse, this model of control and internal competition worked well. But, once global innovation evolved to encompass accessing and integrating dispersed knowledge via collaboration across an agile global innovation footprint, the dual tenets of control and competition became an impediment because they cultivated the following barriers to knowledge transfer and integration:

- *Projector mind-set.* This barrier occurs in an organization in which control lies firmly at the center. Knowledge flows one way, from the center outward as and only when deemed necessary (naturally, by the center). There are essentially two types of projector organizations: The first takes a one-size-fits-all approach; the center dispatches innovations across various markets without concern for local variation. The second type follows a project-and-adapt model in which the center sends innovations to local sites that then make the necessary adaptations for the local market. In neither model is the center willing to learn from or collaborate with local sites and subsidiaries at the periphery.

- *Internal markets.* In organizations that thrive on internal markets and competition, there is usually a lack of trust among divisions, teams, and sites. When people regard other units in the organization as a threat to their own jobs, rewards, and security, the result will be a culture that spurns collaboration and knowledge sharing.

- *Not-invented-here syndrome.* There is a long-held and understandable tradition in the fields of invention, R&D, and innovation that knowledge needs to be protected via patents and copyrights. Often reinforced by organizational structures that separate businesses with their individual profit and loss statements into competing entities for budget and control, this tradition cultivates a culture in which knowledge is excessively hoarded and protected. This phenomenon is commonly referred to as the "not invented here" (NIH) syndrome: when an organization's culture promotes internal competition and rewards individuals and teams on their "original" output, there is no incentive to reuse or share knowledge. When knowledge comes from elsewhere in the organization, people see it as undermining their own or their team's efforts and will consequently often dismiss it, even if its adoption and adaptation could save time and money and provide a better solution.

Dismantling a culture that rejects knowledge sharing is a prerequisite for overcoming the other barriers to freeing knowledge. Tools, mechanisms, and processes that enable companies to connect nodes in a network, bridge different contexts, and transfer and integrate complex knowledge all have to be underpinned by a genuine openness and willingness to share and reuse knowledge. The next chapter describes solutions to each of the barriers, beginning with the vital task of building a culture of reciprocity.

CHAPTER FIVE

Improving Receptivity and Communication

Most of the barriers outlined in the previous chapter are familiar ones. Cumulatively, these barriers can seriously debilitate a company's ability to innovate. But however daunting they may seem, they are not insurmountable. This chapter highlights some of the tools, processes, and mechanisms that a company can employ to facilitate the rich communication and receptivity required for global innovation.

Receptivity: A Prerequisite for Knowledge Transfer and Integration

Only a significant shift in culture toward openness equips organizations to be truly global innovators. Although this type of change challenges long-held orthodoxies and usually meets resistance, there are ways to force change without creating too much turbulence within a company. Take the example of Xerox's R&D organization outlined in sidebar 5-1. In 2000, Xerox began a journey that would transform it over the following decade from a highly secretive culture to one of genuine openness, collaboration, and receptivity.

SIDEBAR 5-1

XEROX: FROM A CULTURE OF SECRECY TO OPEN KNOWLEDGE SHARING AND REUSE

For many decades, Xerox's competitive advantage was based on a handful of technology patents. This culture translated into one of secrecy and knowledge hoarding in which people believed that if they shared knowledge, they eroded value.

In early 2000, French Xerox engineer Laurent Julliard, who had been deeply involved in Linux, authored a white paper on the potential of open source approaches for Xerox. At the time, Xerox's four thousand software engineers were producing around 10 million lines of code each year. Julliard thought Xerox needed to learn how to share and reuse code to leverage this asset. He saw an opportunity to bring about culture change in Xerox and began by positioning open source as a cost-efficiency measure with a by-product of knowledge sharing.

By the end of 2000, Xerox gave Julliard the go-ahead to form a small team to design and deploy an open source platform globally. The solution, "CodeX," is an intranet-hosted tool that supports code sharing, documentation management, Web site hosting, discussion forums, and bug tracking within an environment that provides a unified architecture across Xerox with common tool kits and project administration tools. When developers set up a new project, it can be hosted on the CodeX platform. The metadata from each project is automatically uploaded to the CodeX global server, and this is logged onto a "yellow pages" so the entire CodeX population can access and search it.

It was paramount to use a platform that would be credible and to choose a system that was easy to use. Xerox chose SourceForge to host its system. It had been created in an open source community but had moved into the commercial arena. Although Xerox adapted the system to meet its own requirements by providing audit trails and external access control, many developers within Xerox were familiar with SourceForge and were immediately comfortable using it in its incarnation as CodeX.

According to Julliard, "The technology is the easy bit." He and his team saw their real challenge in mounting an effective communication and education campaign to bring Xerox's developers onboard. Prior to the launch of CodeX on January 1, 2001, the three-man team gave over a hundred road-show presentations at Xerox sites around the world. While some developers were enthusiastic about adopting this new open way of working, the attitude of a large contingent was summed up by one developer who said that his code was so important to him that he wouldn't even share it with his mother.

CodeX quickly attracted a critical mass of users needed to bring about the community effect. After almost three years, it had fifteen hundred developers and two hundred fifty active projects. In financial terms (and based on conservative estimates of only one in ten downloads being useful), developers had reused the equivalent of $80 million of software code. By 2011,

(continued)

CodeX (now called Codendi) had around forty-three hundred developers registered on its internal site and a further five hundred on the external site it uses for hosting projects with partners.

In the twelve years since Xerox first introduced CodeX as a wedge to force culture change, the firm has changed drastically. The culture of innovation in the firm is now based on collaboration and openness. In addition to Codendi, which is still used internally and for projects with partners, Xerox has opened up its innovations to wider public scrutiny and feedback with its open.xerox site, which lets users test-drive new Xerox technologies.

Knowledge sharing tools can be very effective in forcing culture change through practice. But when embarking on this approach, there are several things to remember:

- *It's about people, not technology.* The process of knowledge sharing and the culture change required to implement it are about people; the best technology in the world will fail if people aren't engaged to use it. The focus should be on communicating the message and educating people about the benefits. Only by using the system will employees recognize its advantages and change their behavior. Take the example of communities of practice. People find that once they have benefited or learned from the community, they will more readily participate. Xerox gave engineers adequate benefits to encourage them to use the new Codendi system.

- *Senior managers need to support the effort.* Engaging users is the key to bringing about culture change, but this doesn't negate the need for clear and visible senior management support to provide legitimacy.

- *Business units need to adapt the rules of ownership.* A lot of knowledge is legally owned by individual business units (either as patents or IP rights). So not only does the company have to encourage a culture of contribution and exchange, but it also has to modify the culture of ownership. If different business units (profit centers) are going to openly share knowledge, then corporate lawyers need to define clear rules with regard to IP usage and reuse from the outset.

- *The approach has to be global.* An open culture cannot be exclusive to a small group of people, a specific set of divisions, or a few geographies. To gain maximum value and benefit, the culture has to be global. Of course, there will always be free riders in an open culture, those people who will happily use knowledge from elsewhere without ever making a contribution themselves. But because the benefits of openly sharing knowledge to the individual, business unit, and organization are so great, these people will be in the minority.

- *Changing culture will take time.* Like any change program, building a new culture around knowledge sharing and receptivity requires a lot of time. In large organizations, this is more likely to be years than months.

Inadequate Connections: Technology Alone Isn't Enough

To recap, a failure to connect nodes in an innovation network can happen at three different levels: First, inadequate IT systems for sharing codified knowledge; second, failure to leverage technology to connect those who hold knowledge with potential recipients to transfer experiential knowledge; and last, the inability to build personal bonds and networks across various locations to transfer and integrate knowledge. While the three problems differ in nature, their solutions all begin with the premise that pivotal to their success is the need for a clear and obvious benefit to the staff using the systems or working with colleagues at distant sites. Staff should feel that the value gained from using the mechanisms and processes, is greater than the burden of work imposed by having them. In other words, people tend to be more amenable to supporting any system or process if they can recognize the value it adds to their own work experience.

Transferring Codified Knowledge via ICT Systems

Many companies have huge knowledge databases that are a repository or historical record of the company's explicit knowledge. Few people would dare to venture into these systems in the hope of finding current data or information. But systems for codified knowledge can be relevant and add real value if they are designed to be a ubiquitous part of everyday workflow. Citibank Singapore, for instance, created an e-workplace portal to improve customer service in fifteen local regions by replacing the numerous independent systems that didn't talk to each other. It created one portal that enabled staff in different locations and product groups, such as foreign exchange, equities, structured finance, and so on, to share analytical tools and client profiles. This move from knowledge silos of individual products and countries to knowledge available about all of Citibank's product areas in the region empowered employees with a better understanding of client needs.

But to be successful, Citibank recognized that the e-workplace shouldn't be about technology, but about how people create, store, access, and deploy explicit knowledge. So to encourage staff across Asia to upload and download information from the system, it designed the e-workplace to be part of the workflow and linked it to the balanced scorecard. As a result, the system was widely adopted and used, providing Citibank with a valuable tool for sharing client knowledge across all of its businesses in the region.

Leveraging IT Systems to Connect Knowledge Holders

IT systems that support knowledge sharing don't have to be limited to the storage and retrieval of codified knowledge such as technical databases, management information systems, or even the type of workplace portal developed by Citibank Singapore. By leveraging existing intranet platforms, a company can establish communities of practice (CoPs) that provide an effective, yet low-cost mechanism for individuals or teams to reach out to a wider community of experts within an organization to seek experiential knowledge. For years, researchers have observed that groups of people with a shared interest form communities outside the bounds of organizational structures.[1] These CoPs can connect people, teams, and sites across a dispersed organization, particularly in the area of problem solving.

Many companies that have experimented with CoPs have failed to gain any real value from them, despite their huge potential to speed up and streamline problem solving by linking knowledge seekers with knowledge holders. Yet they offer a potentially powerful tool for sharing experiential knowledge, as long as they are set up and managed based on the following principles:

- *CoPs should be small and focused.* CoPs don't require universal adoption to be effective. In fact, communities that have many participants are in danger of becoming global debating societies rather than forums focused on problem solving in specific areas. The best CoPs work by identifying and involving key knowledge holders. When problems or questions are posted to the community, each person then taps his or her own personal network to find a solution or relevant experience that might help. Keeping CoPs small and focused builds stronger commitment between members (as every member is known and accountable) and allows greater agility because there is clarity in roles and areas of expertise.

- *People don't collaborate for collaboration's sake.* CoPs need to have a legitimate purpose, a raison d'être that focuses on solving specific types of problems. The CoP can be a tool that adds genuine value by attracting relevant knowledge and expertise from around a dispersed organization. But it won't work unless the people using and sponsoring it see the benefit: members of the community should gain fast problem solving, professional development, and networking opportunities. Once momentum gathers, the personal and professional benefits reinforce commitment. But in the early days of a CoP, when community members are building trust, they need to publicize success stories to reinforce the value of CoP activity.

- *CoPs have no dollar value.* The value created by CoPs is difficult to measure by any defined metrics. While there are some crude measures such as, "number of new ideas taken to experiment stage" or "number of problems solved," these are never going to capture all activity across a global network nor can they measure the value of the CoPs' network building.

- *CoPs shouldn't be silos.* While CoPs can be very effective in sharing knowledge globally within their own domain, they can themselves become knowledge silos, isolated from the core organization and other communities.[2] To avoid this, a company needs to have mechanisms in place to connect CoPs. Oversight groups can bring together representatives from different CoPs. Groupwide newsletters and bulletin boards can publicize the work of various CoPs, for example, by listing the big topic areas that are current within a given community and illustrating some solutions they have put forward and adopted. Within any organization, different business groups or functions can unknowingly share similar problems that their own CoPs are working to resolve. Connecting CoPs across businesses and functions creates a wider web of connections to share knowledge and solve problems more effectively and efficiently.

Building Networks to Connect Nodes

Critical to an integrated global innovation network are teams and divisions that are conduits for knowledge transfer and learning. Team members need to understand what is happening at other sites and why. They should feel they are first and foremost part of a global activity (an individual project or ongoing development) rather than part of the site where they are physically located. But expecting people to step out of their own shoes everyday and into those of someone who is very different and distant is expecting a lot. Most people naturally favor the path of least resistance—to stick with what is familiar, comfortable, and close to home. Few people will, of their own accord, establish lines of communication and build bonds with peers in different locations.

As connections across sites become a more important aspect of transferring knowledge that is increasingly dispersed, a company can adopt mechanisms to promote the ongoing interaction needed for wider connectivity. The example of Synopsys described in sidebar 5-2 provides a good illustration of how a company can engineer connectivity between different locations with different cultures. The odds for successful knowledge transfer and integration seemed stacked against Synopsys, with vital embedded knowledge imprisoned by distance, organizational structures and cultures, national norms and culture, various languages, and different knowledge bases.

SIDEBAR 5-2

SYNOPSYS: CONNECTING DISPERSED TEAMS

Synopsys is one of the world's leaders in electronic design automation (EDA), software that automates the translation of semiconductor design ideas into solutions. Recognizing the potential in specialist areas like electronic modeling and digital signal processing (DSP) design in growth industries such as mobile telecommunications, Synopsys acquired the German DSP specialist, Cadis.

Immediately after the acquisition, plans were underway to develop a next-generation version of Cadis's main product, COSSAP, which had been extremely successful in Europe but lacked a market in the United States. The solution of how to assign work on the new product between Cadis in Aachen, Germany, and Synopsys in Mountain View, California, was far from obvious. The Cadis engineers had the deep expertise and years of experience

---

in creating real applications for customers for the new product. They also had the knowledge required to keep working on COSSAP until its replacement was launched. But they lacked the resources to work on both versions, and keeping all DSP development and knowledge in Aachen would create a serious barrier to integration between the two firms. At the same time, Synopsys engineers in the United States had no practical experience in the DSP field and so couldn't work on COSSAP or lead the development of its replacement.

Synopsys decided that the incremental development work on COSSAP would stay in Aachen, and the new product development would be carried out by a joint team split between Mountain View and Aachen. A potential problem was that as COSSAP was phased out, the developers working on it in Aachen might feel disenfranchised, as they had not been part of the new product development team.

Based on T. J. Allen's findings that proximity encourages "knowledge flows,"[3] the lab in Aachen was not reorganized around the two different teams. Instead COSSAP and the new product were literally developed side-by-side. This proximity encouraged informal knowledge sharing, and by the time the new product was ready to launch, every member of the team in Aachen who had been working on the old product also had a thorough understanding of its successor.

The development teams at Aachen and Mountain View had very different cultures, and bringing them together to form a virtual team posed potential problems. To build a sense of one team from the two disparate sites, Synopsys arranged a series of onsite assignments. All developers working on the new product spent between four to five weeks working at the other site. Not

(*continued*)

only did this breed familiarity and build informal buddy networks, but each engineer acted as a relay for transferring embedded knowledge between the sites. In addition, Joachim Kunkel, one of the founders of Cadis, relocated to Synopsys so that he could lobby for Cadis and plan and manage the bridges between the two R&D teams.

Synopsys also needed to find a formal reason to keep its dispersed teams talking, which it achieved through a dense web of cross-site and cross-function reporting structures. The structures served both to disentangle the sense of team from place in the early days and ensure that the bridges between the two locations were cemented and strong as time passed. After three years, this complex reporting structure had served its purpose. The two teams were fully integrated.

The success Synopsys experienced in connecting its dispersed teams wasn't only due to the structures and processes it put in place. Its cosmopolitan managers played a critical role in overcoming the problem of transferring knowledge between different contexts. These people had lived and worked in different cultures, which gave them an awareness of the different contexts between the knowledge source and the location in which the knowledge would be integrated. They had the ability to see things from another and often very different perspective and were much less likely to fall victim to miscommunication and misinterpretation between locations. In the foraying activities described in chapter 2, scouts played this role. In the case of Synopsys, the cosmopolitan managers were multicultural team members from both sites acting as bicultural relays.

Communicating Across Different Contexts:
Imposing a Common Language

Communication barriers created by different functions, national languages, culture, and organizational structures result in companies fragmented by multiple contexts—the personal, professional, behavioral, local, and so forth. The paradox is that these different contexts add value to the innovation process, providing a rich tapestry of inputs. So companies face a challenge in overcoming the fragmentation that results from multiple contexts while at the same time having to maintain the richness and diversity of knowledge those multiple contexts provide. In scenarios where the knowledge that needs to be exchanged and integrated is embedded or explicit, adopting a common language provides an effective method for achieving this. By common language, we refer to the universal adoption of tools and processes to drive and support the innovation process. These tools can be put together piecemeal or, when the product architecture is modular, the goals are clearly defined, and the innovation is incremental, the company can adopt a system such as "design for six sigma" (DFSS). DFSS, part of the quality movement, focuses on efficiency and creates robust products, while imposing a common language, vocabulary, and shared experience across an organization.

The main benefit of this approach is its universality in bringing together people from various parts of a firm and providing a common structure, road map, templates, analytical tools, metrics, and feedback mechanisms, regardless of function or location. Differences are not swept aside, but are considered valuable contributions within a broader common and inclusive framework. Siemens used DFSS to impose a common language across various parts of its organization in order to support the development new products in China (see sidebar 5-3).

SIDEBAR 5-3

SIEMENS: DFSS, A TOOL TO IMPOSE A COMMON LANGUAGE

For many years, Siemens had been manufacturing mobile phones at its plant in Shanghai. But as its business in China grew, the need to move development closer to customers in Asia and the opportunity to tap the emerging engineering talent pool became apparent. In response, Siemens opened a design center in Beijing to focus on adapting existing products to suit local market requirements. Within a year, it was clear to managers in Munich that the group's R&D capacity in Europe was stretched to its limits by the demands for constant new product releases. They decided to give the Beijing center its first new product design mandate, the A55.

The A55 had to be completed in the same six-month development cycle as all other mobile phones. But moving the design of the A55 to China was a sizable risk: while the Beijing center had proved very adept at adapting mobiles to meet local manufacturing and market requirements, it had no experience in designing a new product and much of the knowledge it needed was dispersed across different functions in Europe.

Siemens needed a way to bring together virtually the relevant specialists from Europe with the development team in Beijing to work on the A55. It chose to adopt "design for six sigma" (DFSS). The goal of the six sigma strategy is to perfect any process so that there are no more than 3.4 defects per million. Its offshoot, DFSS, provides a collection of factual data tools, statistical measurement, feedback mechanisms, metrics to evaluate the design, processes, and the discipline to allow virtual teams to work together with clear goals, a common language, and transparent management accountability.

Siemens broke down the development of the A55 into modules or subsystems ("critical modules" in DFSS terminology). Each of the critical modules had two teams: a cross-functional team including someone from quality, manufacturing, procurement, and design; and a specialist team with one member who also worked with the cross-functional team. The cross-functional team was responsible for the continual analysis of the design from the viewpoint of its own functional perspectives. This analysis provided the beginning of a learning record of why decisions were made, and also integrated the areas of specialist knowledge at the beginning of the design process.

As the project progressed, the entire A55 team began to share a common vocabulary and understanding based on the DFSS tools it had been using. All team members were trained to use a new tool before it was introduced to support part of the project. No one was excluded from this process, so as a team, they began to develop a shared experience, understanding, and vocabulary. This shared language was further entrenched by monthly presentations at which each team discussed its findings and progress with the senior management control board. At these meetings, the members spoke as the team for a particular critical module, not as acoustics engineers, manufacturing engineers, and so on. The language they used to describe their challenges was the language of analysis from the tools they had employed. In a short time, DFSS had created a uniform context across geographical and functional boundaries.

(continued)

The A55 project was the first time that Siemens had brought together people with different skills, experience, and perspectives to work on a product design. Not only did this project support the integration of various functional elements from the outset, it also resulted in a wide pool of ideas being fed into the design process. For example, for the first time, a manufacturing person could point out, at the design stage, why a certain feature wasn't feasible either because it would require retooling the production line or because it would be too intricate for assembly by hand. It wouldn't necessarily occur to an engineer in Germany, used to designing for automated assembly lines, that manual assembly on China's production lines would present very different manufacturing challenges, many of which could be designed out in the development phase.

In just six months, the A55 teams had developed a robust, reliable product, which was a success in business terms (field rate returns were down by a factor of almost five to the industry average). Furthermore, the thorough training all teams had received throughout the project and the fact they had worked in cross-functional teams meant that they shared a common language, context, and understanding that allowed them to work together and share knowledge in subsequent projects.

As with any process that seeks to change behavior, the only way to instill a common language across a diverse and dispersed organization is through practice. This means making a significant investment in training people with the skills to use the tools, process, and systems that enforce that language. A company needs to make a conscious effort to provide opportunities for people to work together and encourage collaborative projects. This position isn't easy to maintain, because dispersed projects are inherently more difficult to manage than colocated ones. (Chapter 6 looks in detail at the capabilities and structures required for dispersed projects.) But a language that isn't used regularly can quickly become rusty or redundant.

Although tools like DFSS are useful in developing a common language, they are not the perfect solution to integrating knowledge across all innovation activities. By creating a common understanding based on a strict and strongly analytical approach, the scope of the language being created has obvious limitations. This may be fine for incremental innovations based on technical, embedded, or explicit knowledge, but is entirely inappropriate for transferring the type of rich, rooted, complex knowledge required for architectural or creative innovations.

Transferring and Integrating Complex Knowledge: The Role of Cosmopolitan Managers

Potentially the most valuable, complex knowledge is also the most difficult to transfer and integrate because it is rooted and diffuse. Whereas the other barriers to transferring knowledge can be largely surmounted by the clever and creative deployment of existing tools and processes, complex knowledge calls for an entirely new approach: critical to the success of transferring, absorbing, and integrating this knowledge is the role of cosmopolitan managers. These people have experience in living or working in different countries. They have a deep appreciation for and understanding of the subtleties of different social norms, behavior, and beliefs that shape the contexts of knowledge creation and absorption. They act as bridges between these various contexts. But, as we outlined in the previous chapter, our survey showed that few companies proactively develop this type of manager.

Identifying and Developing Cosmopolitan Managers

Managers at Philips had an old saying: in order to have a promising executive career, you needed to start by selling radios in Uganda or Zambia and washing machines in Tierra del Fuego. This wasn't just about testing stamina and creativity in difficult places. Exposing people to frontline roles in different contexts is important for building the capabilities cosmopolitan managers need. Only through immersion in different contexts can people develop the skills for being receptive to the absorption and transfer of complex knowledge.

Emerging markets play a crucial role, because they are so different that it's difficult to ignore context. Take the approach of Singapore-based Olam International in developing cosmopolitan managers. Since its founding in 1989, the globally integrated agricultural and foodstuff supply chain manager has grown rapidly, posting revenues of S$15.7 billion in 2011. One reason for its success is its large cadre of cosmopolitan managers. In many ways, Olam's management ranks more closely resemble a foreign service than a corporate entity. It has over five hundred managers from all over the world who are part of the global assignee talent pool and spend their careers moving between different countries and product groups, often living in remote rural locations in Africa, Asia, and South America. For example, a career might encompass managing cocoa supply in Benin, processing cashews in Tanzania, setting up a coffee plantation in Laos, building a processed food business in Nigeria, as well as running a cotton production business in Australia. As a result, Olam's managers are culturally sensitive, deeply understand multiple contexts, and are able to transfer and meld knowledge to create innovative services, processes, and businesses.

Developing cosmopolitan managers, however, is time consuming and difficult. But most firms already have people with a natural propensity for this role. Finding and using employees who are naturally cosmopolitan and who have grown up or been educated in different countries, for instance, makes sense. These people tend to have contextual awareness and what is sometimes called "frame switching," the ability to consciously shift from one cultural frame to another (for example, to move between a culture of guilt typical of the Judeo-Christian tradition and one of shame typical of a Confucian heritage). Not only are bicultural people able to function between the cultures with which they are familiar, but their unique cross-cultural skills can make them highly effective in new cultures and environments.

Short of on-the-job exposure, people can become aware of the implications of different contexts via insight trips, which enable them to see the "real" country and culture, not just meet expatriates, partners, and suppliers. For example, a day spent in Tokyo's Akihabara electronics district can reveal more about Japanese customer preferences and suitable marketing approaches than weeks spent analyzing data and reading reports. Similarly, when the knowledge needed for an innovation is located far away, visits and assignments to that location not only help people understand the knowledge in situ, but can sensitize them to different contexts. (See sidebar 5-4 describing how GSK sent staff to California to access a new technology.)

Cosmopolitan managers find it easier to be effective in companies that have adopted a universal culture without suppressing cultural diversity. Perhaps the most critical challenge is for the corporate culture to transcend the founding country's imprint, which may not make sense in other cultures and, if strong, can make everyone outside the home country feel peripheral. Amazon, for instance, faced with the challenge of internationalization and then diversification, built its culture around a handful of universal customer priorities, such as fast delivery, low prices, and customer reviews. It can maintain cultural diversity by recontextualizing these universal principles and values so they are meaningful in the local context. If Disney had adopted the simple universal principle of always "putting the guest" first instead of the culturally specific "service with a smile," it could have avoided some of its failures in Europe that we discussed in the previous chapter.[4]

Companies need to fully embrace the task of building a cadre of cosmopolitan managers, with senior management support and clear HR plans. Talented managers will be reluctant to leave headquarters for overseas assignments if there is evidence the company will overlook or marginalize them while away. Companies that recognize the importance of cosmopolitan managers are those whose businesses have long prospered in diverse markets. Firms like Unilever and HSBC have highly visible international manager programs that are a prerequisite for many senior management roles.

However, some new competitors have also recognized the importance of cosmopolitan managers and are building the structures and programs to develop this new breed of manager. Every year, the Korean firm Samsung, as part of its regional specialist program, sends approximately two hundred young managers to experience and live in different countries. To overcome the cultural prejudices that can fester in expatriate enclaves, the managers spend a year living as locals—learning the language, familiarizing themselves with the country, and working on a local project of their own choosing. After completing this immersion training, they can be deployed anywhere in the firm where they use their regional expertise. While this program began in response to Korea's insular culture by sending managers to developed markets, in the last decade, it has shifted to focusing on emerging markets with strong growth potential. Samsung makes a significant investment in developing these cosmopolitan managers, with their immersion experience costing over $100,000 each in addition to their remuneration.[5]

Building Bridges

Trust is a critical factor for the successful functioning of any team, but even more so when working in new and unfamiliar contexts.[6] Strong bonds of trust are essential between the home base and cosmopolitan managers to ensure that the new knowledge has the credibility to be absorbed and integrated.

HP Labs in India (described in chapter 2) was able to share and integrate new complex knowledge with the wider HP network successfully because of the bridges it built. One of the directors of the Bangalore lab was an Indian based in Palo Alto. She had worked for HP Labs in the United States for many years and recognized that she would add much more value by staying in California to act as a lobbyist and champion for the new lab. Much of what the lab was learning (about the IT needs in a poor, rural country) wouldn't gain traction in the United States without someone to bridge the divide and transcribe the findings in a way that made sense to those at headquarters.

The other director of the lab was an eminent Indian scientist based in India, who provided a depth of local understanding and relationships. He understood how government, universities, and business worked in India and was aware of the practical challenges facing the adoption of any IT-based product or service. He provided a bridge between the Bangalore lab and the environment in India.

HP Labs also appointed an American senior manager, who was based in India. During his career, he had worked in many different functions and businesses within HP in the United States and had also spent time working in Taiwan. Being a research lab, HP Labs India, relied on HP's business units to develop and commercialize the products and services it brought to prototype stage. Because these were so radically different from anything HP had developed before, the American senior manager had an indispensable role as a bridge between the context of rural, poor India and HP's global business units.

This triumvirate of cosmopolitan managers at HP acted as the bridge necessary for constant interaction between the new site, its local environment, and other HP sites. The director in Palo Alto and the senior manager in India were both longtime trusted HP employees, with extended formal and informal networks within the group, while the director in India was a highly respected and trusted member of the local scientific and technical community. This meant that the learning in India wasn't isolated or imprisoned but could be decoupled from the local context, transferred, integrated into, and leveraged by HP.

The failure to have cosmopolitan managers as cultural relays locks knowledge in its local context. When Japanese cosmetics group Shiseido set up a new business in France to break into the global perfumery business, it didn't have any bicultural managers to act as relays. Instead, it ostensibly established a French business that, although successful in its own right, failed to add any value to Shiseido's global innovation capability because the knowledge from the new venture (in marketing, branding, manufacturing, and packaging) remained imprisoned in the French unit.

Understanding When Knowledge Is Complex

Before embarking on any attempt to transfer and integrate new knowledge, a company should look beyond the obvious in order to understand the true nature of the knowledge. When GSK paid nearly $500 million for Affymax, a Silicon Valley–based technology company that had developed an automated system for the synthesis and screening of compounds, senior managers made it clear to everyone in the organization that the acquisition was important and that Affymax knowledge needed to be transferred across GSK's network of R&D labs. At face value, this knowledge was explicit: Affymax had created technology in the form of robots and machines to screen and synthesize compounds. But GSK recognized that the key to the successful integration of the machines into its own drug-delivery process was in accessing the contextual knowledge underpinning their development and application (see sidebar 5-4). This complex knowledge was held by the founders who had the vision for what Affymax could achieve and the multidisciplinary teams that had realized that vision.

SIDEBAR 5-4

GSK AFFYMAX: AN APPROACH FOR INTEGRATING COMPLEX KNOWLEDGE

With the emergence of a plethora of new technologies and approaches challenging traditional pharmaceutical companies, senior managers at GlaxoSmithKline (GSK) felt that the pharmaceutical industry had to change the way it approached drug

(continued)

discovery (the process had changed little since the beginnings of modern medicine). GSK needed to build a portfolio of experimental activities, and while there would be an inherent risk in doing this, GSK thought the risk of inertia would be greater.

One of these experimental technologies was combinatorial chemistry. Traditionally, chemists synthesized compounds one at a time, and then biologists tested them one at a time. The Silicon Valley–based company Affymax saw the potential to speed up this process and developed machines that would automate the process of efficient high-throughput synthesis and screening. To access this new technology, GSK acquired Affymax for $500 million.

The Affymax encoded synthesis library (ESL) machines were not commercially available; consequently it was essential to learn how to build, maintain, and operate them. When a GSK site had an interest in adopting Affymax technology, it would send a group of scientists to Affymax for four to six months. During their time in California, they underwent formal training (and testing) in how to use the technology and build the machines. They also built personal networks within Affymax, which helped integrate the new acquisition into GSK. At the end of their assignment, they disassembled the machines and shipped them back to their own site, ready to be rebuilt back home.

The GSK site in the United Kingdom was the first to transfer the synthesis technology; it took on a consulting role to help other sites within the GSK network. While GSK employees were excited about the new technologies, there was a big difference between seeing them in isolation at Affymax in California and seeing them in a real GSK lab, integrated into the drug-discovery process. So, in addition to assignments at Affymax, employees from Japan,

Italy, Spain, and France all visited the U.K. to see how the Affymax technologies worked within the context of GSK.

For those sites that chose to adopt the Affymax technology, the size of the lab, its resources, and the type of work it focused on had an impact on how it used the new technology. Each site transferred the standard technology and then encouraged its own experts to adapt it to meet their needs through local technology development. So, for example, the North Carolina site adapted the ESL machine to perform parallel synthesis, while Verona adapted the technology to bring the work of chemists and biologists closer together through solid phase synthesis.

Five years after the Affymax acquisition, combinatorial chemistry had matured, and many of the original Affymax technologies had pervaded GSK. Automated parallel synthesis for all types of lead discovery and high-throughput screening were just two of the technologies emerging from combinatorial chemistry, which are now part of the standard armory for drug discovery.

By recognizing that much of the knowledge it sought was, in fact, complex in nature and not explicit, GSK was able to integrate and adapt the knowledge widely across its global R&D network. The U.K. team members that initially went to Affymax to learn about the high-throughput machines and integrate them in their own lab then acted as the vital bridge for integrating the new knowledge into other GSK sites. They understood why and how the machines had been developed and how to adapt and modify them to support GSK's drug development process. Had GSK not recognized the true nature of the knowledge it wanted to transfer and had merely shipped technologies to its labs, it would have been unable to successfully integrate the new technology. And that would have been a very expensive failure.

To meet current and future knowledge needs, companies need a much more strategic approach to the transfer and integration of knowledge; the basic challenges and approaches are outlined in table 5-1. For all the reasons described in appendix 2 (globalization and the emergence of new consumer markets; growing technology complexity and convergence; demographic changes; increasing external demands such as environmental concerns; and offshore outposts and outsourcing), it's highly unlikely that the trends for greater knowledge dispersion and diversity will change. Companies then face two distinct courses of action. On the one hand, they can continue with business as usual, be it the multidomestic model of innovation, with each local site being largely autonomous and focused on the needs of its own region's markets; a transnational model with a distributed footprint, but each business being strongly centered in one country; or an in-house outsourcing model in which innovations originate at the center with local sites completing modules of noncritical work at a low cost and pushing them down to other subsidiaries and divisions for local implementation. Growing competition points to a limited shelf life for companies that choose these options. On the other hand, companies can embrace knowledge diversity and dispersion and build an innovation network that leverages the best, most interesting, and most valuable knowledge from around the world. To be successful, companies need to recognize the current shortcomings in their ability to transfer and integrate knowledge and implement the requisite solutions to conquer them.

Together, the solutions we described for overcoming each of the barriers will transform an organization's ability to

TABLE 5-1

Overcoming the barriers to freeing knowledge

Barriers	Characteristics	Solutions
Lack of receptivity	• Control and internal competition • Projector mind-set • Not invented here	• Knowledge sharing tools as a wedge to force culture change • Knowledge sharing about people not technologies; benefits and training focus • User pull and senior management support • Clear rules of knowledge ownership • Takes time and has to be global
Inadequate connections		
ICT systems for codified knowledge	• Incompatible IT systems • Large database repositories	• Obvious benefits to users • Ubiquitous and integrated into workflow
IT systems to connect knowledge holders	• Isolated experts • Reinventing the wheel	• Leverage existing infrastructure to connect dispersed groups/people • Use as problem-solving tool (obvious benefits to users)
Networks connecting sites and teams	• Extreme localism with lack of interaction between sites	• Dense webs of cross-site reporting and communication • Relays between sites
Multiple different contexts	• Organization structure • Functional languages and world views • Cultures and norms, languages	• Common language, tools, goals, and metrics for embedded and explicit knowledge • Investment in training • Collaborative projects
Transferring and integrating complex knowledge	• Can be difficult to recognize • Inherently difficult to share as rooted in originating context	• Programs to develop cosmopolitan managers as bridges between contexts • Identifying people with natural bicultural skills • Universal corporate values and principles

leverage knowledge and deliver innovations that will build competitive advantage. But individually, each will have an impact on freeing knowledge and changing behavior and expectations. Knowledge management systems designed to bridge divides and focus on integration into the workflow are much more valuable and powerful than those that store data. Mechanisms like CoPs that connect those people who seek knowledge with those who hold it are inexpensive to implement and have the added advantage of building strong networks of people across boundaries that would otherwise be unaware of each others' existence. A concerted effort to integrate teams across different countries brings market and product knowledge as well as experience together to develop more robust products and services. The adoption of a common language can eliminate the problems and limitations imposed by communication barriers and provide a route to successful dispersed project development for incremental innovations. And understanding when knowledge is complex and developing an HR policy to build a cadre of cosmopolitan managers who can act as bicultural relays will better position companies to develop game-changing innovations. All these solutions, to a greater or lesser extent, begin to change behavior through practice and results. But, sometimes, an activity designed to act as a wedge to bring about a change in culture is the only way to build the necessary level of momentum within an organization.

Although a company may encounter resistance, people eventually recognize the personal and professional benefits of a culture that values and promotes openness and receptivity in knowledge transfer and integration. As the boundaries of innovation extend beyond an individual organization to a wider ecosystem involving external parties, a culture that embraces knowledge sharing becomes even more important. In the next part of the book, we examine why communication and receptivity are paramount to setting up and running global innovation projects and how companies can widen their knowledge net further to encompass various types of collaboration with external parties.

PART IV

OPTIMIZING COLLABORATION

Succeeding Globally

CHAPTER SIX

Organizing for Global Innovation Projects

The final leg of our journey prepares and arms companies to compete in an era of global innovation: optimizing collaboration by innovating with partners and managing global innovation projects. These global projects, which involve multiple sites across a network, provide the organizing structure that will leverage footprints, drive integration, and unleash the real value inherent in a dispersed approach to innovation. These projects are the lifeblood that animates and energizes a global footprint.

Global projects create competitive advantage in two ways: First, when the embedded and complex knowledge for innovations comes from multiple sites, it is difficult for competitors to copy those innovations. To do so, they would need to have an identical footprint to access the same knowledge. Second, companies can achieve enormous efficiencies by dividing large and complex innovation projects across multiple sites. Development can take place in parallel, reducing time to market, cutting development costs, and resulting in first-mover advantage.

Yet, despite these benefits, our innovation survey, together with anecdotal evidence, revealed that in reality, even companies with relatively dispersed footprints are currently engaging in very few global projects, and when they do, they find that the benefits fall short of expectations, with projects that are difficult to manage and yield poor results. These failures then drive the wrong learning—that global innovation projects create little value. Whereas, in fact, global projects tend to fail because most companies haven't recognized that they are inherently different from colocated ones. A three-stage process of identification, definition, and delivery ensures the entire innovation process from ideation to product or service rollout melds the best possible knowledge, skills, and capabilities from around the world.

There are a number of prerequisites that a company must meet for its global innovation projects to thrive and deliver their potential. We begin this chapter by describing these prerequisites; many will be unfamiliar in this context because they don't apply to colocated projects. After laying out the conditions essential for project success, we then examine the three phases of global innovation projects—identification, definition, and delivery—and describe how each phase should be organized, the activities it needs to encompass, and any potential pitfalls that may be encountered.

Why Globally Dispersed Projects Fail

Failed or troubled innovation projects are extremely disruptive. They increase costs, lower morale, and can result in damaging delays to market. Yet few companies really understand why global projects fail. Audits may highlight practices that appear to have had an adverse effect on a project, but because they rarely take a systemic view, rectifying these practices has little impact on future project success. In any system, if the environment and infrastructure that provide the foundation and support are lacking or are toxic, the system will break down. The same holds true for global innovation projects. Before the project can get underway, a company has to put the right conditions in place to support it.

An Underlying Lack of Organizational Stability

Certainly the first and perhaps the most crucial question to ask before embarking on a major global innovation project is whether the organization is stable or in flux. The latter bodes ill for the prospect of any global project. When organizations are undergoing periods of change due to restructuring—the integration of new acquisitions or a new top team settling in, for example—management attention is focused on issues bigger than any individual project.

Global innovation projects need senior managers' consistent commitment, yet during periods of major change, they are much more likely to be redeployed to deal with particular trouble spots within the organization. Senior managers champion projects and are responsible for the high-level decision making that can make the difference between project success and failure. Without their continual involvement and constant attention, a global innovation project drifts and loses direction.

To illustrate the impact of an unstable environment on a global project, consider the Apcantes project at a global electronics firm we will refer to as Elecompt, which took place at a time of great instability: not only was the firm integrating new acquisitions, but it was also reorganizing (see sidebar 6-1). Although the Apcantes project was of strategic importance, management focus was understandably elsewhere, leaving critical decisions hanging in the air while the project teams became disenchanted. In this instance, the firm recognized problems before they became terminal and it invested a lot of time and money getting the project back on track. But, for many companies, periods of instability can kill complex, global innovation projects, costing not only millions of dollars but lost potential to get innovative new products or services to market.

SIDEBAR 6-1

APCANTES: A TROUBLED GLOBAL PROJECT

Elecompt's Apcantes project was based on an idea for a new product, a smart technical block (STB) to control machine tools in automated production. By replacing closed technical blocks with networked "island" STBs, the product would offer customers much more choice and flexibility in which devices to connect. Although the Apcantes project represented a strategic shift for Elecompt—from providing customers with integrated solutions to a stand-alone component—the company didn't see it as a large or complex project. In fact, there were three major projects launched at the same time, which took priority for resources and management attention.

Based on resource availability, Apcantes was split between the Lower Saxony site in Germany, which had experience in the field of technical blocks and the Massachusetts site in the

---

United States, which had no previous experience. The project encountered its first problems early on when almost a quarter of the staff, including key project members in Massachusetts, were enticed to join start-ups during the dot-com boom, leaving Massachusetts without mechanical capabilities. The project was now missing a chunk of competencies required for the development of the STB, so a site in Paris, France, was drafted to take over.

The backbone of the STB was the "bus" communications structure. At the beginning of the Apcantes project, Elecompt decided to use a proprietary bus for optimal performance. Nine months after development of the proprietary standard had begun, Elecompt decided to change to an open standard called Can Open, even though the development team in the United States didn't have experience working with this technology. Strategically, this switch made sense because the new product needed to be compatible with competitors' offerings. Unfortunately, the company had never shared the strategic rationale for Apcantes with the project teams, and never explained the decision to adopt Can Open. The teams' morale was seriously affected. Design work had to start again, and because no one at Elecompt had experience with Can Open, it had to outsource this critical part of the project to Wipro in India.

Apcantes had been broken down into modules, but in reality the product structure was highly interdependent. For example, the vibration response changed, depending on the weight of the controllers that were installed on the bases. And the vibration rate was relevant to the electrical connections within the unit, because if vibrations were too high, it could result in broken connections. However, a lack of knowledge overlap at each site meant that none of the sites understood the implications that

(continued)

143

their design and development decisions would have on the other parts of the project.

The integration problems were exacerbated by a lack of global project experience and poor communication between sites. Language presented a particular hurdle because the general level of English among the French team members was very poor and the native English speakers in Massachusetts did not realize how little of their colloquial English was understood at the other sites.

The relationship with Wipro in India, managed from the United States, presented more challenges: with no experience with Can Open, their oversight role was all but impossible. The time difference between India and the East Coast of the United States meant there was no overlap in the workday and, consequently, communication was very limited. Eventually, the German team took over the management of Wipro. Time differences were easier to manage, and it also had the necessary software experience to oversee and guide Wipro.

Perhaps because Elecompt never envisaged Apcantes as a complex project, there was minimal project management and coordination across sites. Frictions developed between the sites based on personality clashes and a general lack of trust. According to Jim Morrison, head of engineering and quality, "Everything was always late and we kept discovering new problems. Escalation of problems took place, but it was very difficult to get an escalation of commitments. It was a constant battle to make sure enough resources were dedicated to the project, and our main role was firefighting."

This lack of direction largely stemmed from the absence of senior leadership. The Apcantes steering committee did not meet regularly, and when it did, few members attended. Their attention was focused on the bigger projects that were running at the time, and as a result, the small problems Apcantes initially encountered snowballed into large problems. Almost two years into the project, senior managers finally recognized that Apcantes was in serious trouble. They hired specialist consultants to introduce processes and systems to Apcantes and build a global work schedule. Despite the myriad problems that had plagued the development, when Apcantes was finally launched, the project teams delivered a very good product, albeit late and over budget.

Too Little Trust Between Sites

Organizations used to running colocated innovation projects for the most part take trust for granted. When people work together every day, they are cognizant of each other's commitment, ability, integrity, and ethical codes. This allows them to function effectively and confidently as a team. But this is not the case for dispersed teams. That distance and unfamiliarity are impediments to trust has been well documented.[1]

Without trust between dispersed team members, projects will struggle to deliver anything. Teams need to have faith that the other project teams have sufficient competencies and skills to complete their part of the task successfully and on time; they need to trust that expert advice is valid and that decisions are sound; they need to trust that the members of other teams are pulling their weight and committed to delivering the best possible solutions on time. This level of trust isn't something that just happens at the beginning of a project; it needs to build over time through smaller collaborative engagements between the teams.

No Shared Strategic Context

Sharing the strategic context driving an innovation with the people who will be working on the project makes logical sense. Unless people understand why the project is happening, what it is supposed to achieve both strategically for the organization and for customers, and what market the innovation is targeting, they won't be equipped to make the right decisions during the development process.

Unfortunately, this high-level strategic and marketing rationale is commonly lost once the project planning process gets underway and the focus shifts to schedules, milestones, and budgets. If the strategic context isn't shared, each site will impose its own assumptions on the purpose of the project, resulting in inevitable conflicts, fragmentation, and an end result that doesn't meet the strategic requirements of the project.

Overreliance on ICTs

There has been much hype over the ability of ICTs to shrink the world, cut travel costs, and support round-the-clock virtual teamwork. While ICTs have undoubtedly revolutionized the way we work and communicate, they have serious limitations that become all too apparent in global innovation projects. When teams are separated not only by geography but by culture, social norms, and language, ICTs can add to the confusion and miscommunication as they magnify differences. When ICTs are the primary means of communication and collaboration in global innovation projects, they inevitably lead to project failure.

The development of new products or services relies on the melding of embedded, complex knowledge. As discussed in the previous chapter, this melding cannot be achieved via ICTs but requires personal interactions and a strong reliance on cosmopolitan managers. In the context of a project, this means face-to-face visits and onsite assignments. If the company hasn't planned and budgeted for such visits, it will be impossible to share critical rooted, context-dependent knowledge.

Too Much Time Doing and Not Enough Time Planning

When facing complex and costly global innovation projects, a company may be tempted to start the development as quickly as possible. But studies have shown a positive correlation between project success and an investment in defining goals and technical specifications.[2] It takes time to achieve management buy-in, identify and resolve potential problems, and plan project goals, process flows, time lines, interfaces, and knowledge requirements.

A failure to invest adequate time and resources in defining a project up front invariably results in greater costs as the project gets underway. The company will spend valuable time and resources firefighting problems when they arise, resulting in time overruns, loss of morale, spiraling costs, and all too often, project failure.

Global Innovation Projects: Success in Three Phases

When global innovation projects originate at the center and work packages are allocated to various sites in the network, we can easily see how the factors that lead to project failure come into play. As figure 6-1 illustrates, instead of addressing dispersion merely at the point of dividing up work, global innovation projects should embrace dispersion from the start. Successful global projects are divided into three distinct phases, which are inclusive and tap the global innovation footprint:

- *Identification.* In this phase, a company makes sense of the confluence of emerging technologies and market trends to define new opportunities and develop embryonic product or service concepts. This phase is where ideas and experiments are born. Knowledge needs to be accessed from around the world, both internally and externally. However, this phase differs from the identification phase of a colocated project in that the people contributing and making sense of the knowledge are from different parts of the organization (both functions and geographies). As such, they bring a richness of different experiences, knowledge, and capabilities to the project.

- *Definition.* Most companies would refer to this as the pre-project phase. The project is defined in terms of product architecture, budgets, allocation of work packages, identification of subcontractors, articulation of goals, and agreement on systems and process. But in addition to these familiar tasks, companies must undertake a number of other activities: an assessment of organizational stability; a decision on reporting structures both within the project and between the project and organization; details on interfaces and interdependencies; decisions on communication and collaboration channels; and evaluation of capabilities and experience at each site to confirm that the requisite competencies are in place to deliver each part of the project.

- *Delivery.* By this phase, the company should have articulated the problem and solution. Delivery is concerned with running and managing the project, bringing it in on time, on budget, and to specification.

It requires heavyweight project management with dense communication channels not only internally but also with subcontractors and partners and strong leadership from both the project management team and senior management.

Each phase in the global project life cycle calls for different management approaches and coordination and integration processes. But a common seam running through the entire project is inclusion. During the identification phase, a company harnesses diversity to provide valuable insights and inputs from around the world. By involving all of the proposed project teams in the definition phase, it identifies and resolves potential design and compatibility problems before the project launch, forms informal networks, and establishes a shared view of the product architecture and project goals. By the time the delivery phase is underway, a global project team is in place, as opposed to dispersed teams working on a project.

FIGURE 6-1

The three phases of global projects

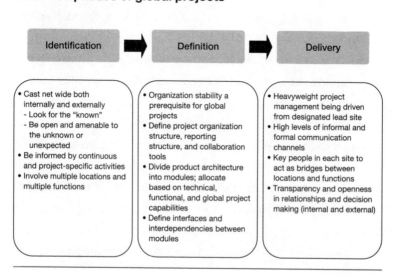

149

Identification: From Idea to Concept

Global innovation projects start by identifying opportunities, forming ideas, and developing concepts. This process of identification needs to be globally inclusive because good ideas for innovation are just as likely to come from the other side of the world—where customer requirements vary, orthodoxies may differ, or regulations impose different restrictions, for example—as from the home base. Having a distinct identification phase ensures that the best ideas and knowledge inputs are gathered from around the world.

Continuous and Project-Specific Identification

Identification activities take place at two different levels: continuous and project specific. Continuous identification spots emerging needs, potential new markets, or the opportunity for new and different business models. We have already looked in detail at the activities and processes that constitute continuous identification in chapters 2 and 5, with attracting, foraying, and experiencing and the mechanisms for integrating the new knowledge these activities yield.

Fledgling projects also need to access specific knowledge so they can graduate from idea to concept. A good project identification phase taps as many diverse and dispersed sources as possible. When Citibank Singapore developed its e-workplace portal, it didn't only look to other sites in the region to flesh out its embryonic idea but went much farther afield. Internally, it found that similar ideas (although much less ambitious in scope) were being developed at the Mexico and Brazil sites. From these, it was able to borrow and adapt the concept of instant collaboration to enable product specialists and account managers to price products for customers. External identification activities led to a critical piece of knowledge in developing the tool—that the success of the initiative wouldn't just depend on technology, but on how information was created, stored, accessed, and deployed. Had the project team not cast its net so wide during the identification phase, Citibank Singapore would have missed valuable knowledge that contributed to defining the functionality and philosophy behind its highly successful e-workplace portal.

The Importance of Dialogue and Building Trust

Ambiguity and uncertainty in motives and roles can beset the early phases of a global project. When sites have competed in the past, strong rivalries can remain that color interpretation and lead to false assumptions drawn from even the most innocent comments, statements, or decisions. The transparency and ongoing dialogue that are critical for building trust throughout a project have to be rooted in the identification phase so that people openly explore assumptions and build common ground. This means communicating the strategic rationale driving the project to everyone involved and being clear in defining early on the roles and responsibilities for the project life cycle. This is easier to achieve when each team brings unique knowledge to the project with a small degree of overlap to support interaction.[3]

Building trust between people and teams worldwide is difficult and takes time. But there are some steps that a company can take to expedite this process and bring about the levels of unity necessary for global projects: First, it's easier to build trust in stable environments that support routines. So it's important to follow the script and not improvise or do unexpected things. Developing routines that reinforce this predictability is helpful. For example, at a basic level, think about taking the train to work. For those of us who don't live in war-torn countries, the train operator usually gets us to work on time. However, if the operators started randomly changing the time table without notice or closing the track for maintenance, our trust in them would rapidly diminish.

Second, communication delays can be a source of confusion that may breed unwarranted suspicion. It's easy to overcome this by quickly responding when problems arise, even if that response just spells out why a full answer will be delayed. Next, being sensitive to the risk of false attribution can prevent small actions from escalating into personal slights. When someone misses a key meeting or fails to send something he or she has been working on, don't blame the individual without first checking the context; illness, accidents, or technology failures could be the cause. This may seem an obvious point, but people can easily lose sight of the obvious when under pressure. Finally, if conflicts do arise, do not engage in a war of narratives to attribute blame but acknowledge differences in perspectives and priorities. (See table 6-1 for a summary of the identification phase.)

Definition: Defining, Detailing, and Planning

After the concept, basic functionality, and purpose of the innovation are outlined in the identification phase, the project definition can get underway. There are so many interrelated variables at play in global projects that the complexity is immense. Although it's impossible to plan for all eventualities, a company can avoid costly delays and fatal errors by first defining and planning the crucial structural and process elements of the project. So we reiterate the importance of taking time to work on the project definition.

TABLE 6-1

The identification phase

What to do	What not to do
• Think of identification in terms of ongoing and project-specific activities	• Don't keep creative thinking and new product planning in your home base or multidomestic hubs
• Involve your global innovation network in ideation; widen the net as far as possible to tap potential global customers, suppliers, and partners as well as internal sites	• Don't confine identification to narrow parameters; this can result in overlooking or ignoring critical knowledge
• Open a dialogue to explore assumptions, build common ground, and ensure trust between sites	
• Begin to build a shared context around the purpose of the innovation and its target customer group	
• Start to outline ideas for basic functionality	

Some of the same tasks familiar in the preplanning of colocated projects, such as budgeting, setting milestones, breaking down the product architecture into workable modules, and defining the interfaces and interdependencies between them, still need to be done during the definition phase of a global project. But there are two additional areas that require significant attention when a project is dispersed: staffing the project and establishing communication channels.

Staffing Global Projects

Most firms under relentless pressure to achieve efficiencies may be tempted to see global innovation projects as a means to most efficiently use dispersed resources by allocating people to projects on the basis of staff availability. But this availability-based resourcing model ignores a fundamental tenet of global innovation, that every site in an innovation network should contribute its distinctive and unique capabilities. There is little point in having differentiation if it isn't leveraged in innovation projects.

A Capability-Based Approach

Projects should be staffed by teams with the most suitable capabilities and experience in the domains required for the project. Contrast the examples of the Apcantes and ATV-71 projects (described in sidebars 6-1 and 6-2). As we have seen, the former followed an availability-based resourcing model and assigned a significant part of the development to a site in the United States that had the people available to work on the project, but little experience in that particular field. Consequently, the U.S. team struggled not only with the development but also with the communication with other teams and subcontractors. ATV-71 experienced none of these problems because it followed a capability-based resourcing model, with each site selected for its expertise and the unique knowledge it could contribute to the development.

SIDEBAR 6-2

ATV-71: A SUCCESSFUL DISPERSED PROJECT

Schneider Toshiba Inverter (STI) was formed by a joint venture between Schneider's motion and drives (M&D) business and Toshiba in 1996. Today, it's a global leader with a market share of almost double that of its nearest rival. But in the early days of the new partnership, management commitment to the joint venture wasn't mirrored with acceptance from engineers in

---

France or Japan. To overcome this, STI's management brought the teams together to work on a series of small projects. As Kazushi Ichimura, president of Schneider Toshiba Inverter, explained, "This built trust and even after the first project, both teams began to recognize the value the other brought."

The ATV-71 project was the first global product range STI developed. It was a new range of drives with open communications and a menu of a hundred and fifty applications, including constant torque for conveyors and lifts, variable torque for pumps, and high-performance motion drives. The customer would be able to program the drive via an integrated keypad in any language.

STI estimated that by distributing the project, it could cut development time by two years. The teams involved in ATV-71 were distributed across four countries, France Japan, Austria, and New Zealand. While three of the sites had previously collaborated, the New Zealand site was a recent acquisition and had not worked with any of the other project teams.

The R&D leaders from each of the four sites met to define the product architecture using a decision matrix to ensure that all critical features were taken into account. For example, the Austrian team, which had expertise in high-power devices, pointed out that the control block was a critical component at its end of the product range, so the team made product architecture decisions to ensure that this component would be as risk-free as possible.

To take advantage of each site's specific areas of expertise, the project was divided by level of power. The site in France was responsible for the common control unit. It also had overall responsibility for the project and coordinating global project management. According to Elie Belbel, the head of M&D, "when

(continued)

embarking on a project, you need rules for everything. You can't give people the opportunity to do things differently." So the STI management committee defined responsibilities and communicated them to everyone involved in the project.

Senior managers in STI had an involved hands-on approach to projects. During the ATV-71 project, they participated in team meetings and reviews and engaged in day-to-day decision making. Nowhere was this clearer than at the New Zealand site. Here the team had a different way of working, an entirely different tool set, and had no personal networks with the other sites to fall back on. STI appointed a veteran of M&D as president of the new acquisition. His expatriate roles, including over five years in Japan and over three years in Singapore setting up an R&D center, gave him the expertise to steer the New Zealand site through its first global project.

Buy-in from team members was important, so communication channels included everyone working on ATV-71. Along with regular video meetings, generous travel budgets allowed for face-to-face meetings and a high level of temporary colocation. For example, when the first samples were ready, teams from each site went to Japan, which was leading the quality process, to see how testing was done.

Shortly after the joint venture was formed, STI's management committee had outlined a clear strategic direction for working with subcontractors and defined core capabilities that had to remain internal. Of the five subcontractors who worked on ATV-71, all but one had experience working with STI. Having worked on various projects over the preceding two years, the subcontractors understood not only STI's tools and processes but also its products.

Three years after the project began, the ATV-71 range was launched on schedule. The project had come in on budget at a cost of €40 million, and the product experienced high acceptance rates globally.

Build a Competence in Dispersed Working

Capability-based resource allocation alone won't ensure that dispersed teams are able to work together effectively. Managing and working in global projects require a new set of competencies that need to be learned and practiced: individuals and teams must trust in each other's capabilities, integrity, commitment, and ethical codes; they need to learn how to communicate and work over time differences; and they need to understand the varying nuances of other cultures.

This preparation all takes time, and as many studies have revealed, team performance improves through practice.[4] So the ability to work in global innovation projects can only come about through repeated exposure to dispersed collaboration. Companies can begin to build a competence in dispersed working by giving teams small projects to work on together before their involvement in a major project. It's not necessary for all teams to have worked with every other team prior to a project, but if none of the teams have worked together before, then combining them to work on a major global innovation project for the first time will be too much of a stretch.

Build in a Competence Overlap Between Sites

While sites are selected based on their unique capabilities, there also has to be some overlap of competency between sites. Without overlap, the teams won't understand the impact of interdependencies between the various work packages, making integration very difficult and, in some cases, impossible. For instance, in Apcantes the mechanical elements were developed in France, the electronics in the United States, and software in Germany. But the lack of mechanical competencies in the United States and electronic competencies in France meant that neither site understood the interdependencies between the modules they were developing. For example, electrical connections would break if the vibration rates were too high. While this was blatantly obvious to the electronics team in the United States, the team in France, which developed the mechanics and casing, was unaware of the vibration problem and designed a module that caused strong vibrations. The error was discovered late in the project, and rectifying it resulted in delays and increased costs. All this could have been avoided if there had been an overlap in competencies at each site, with the French team having some electronics capabilities, and the U.S. team, some mechanical expertise.

Establishing Communication Channels

Teams that have built a competence for dispersed working have stronger informal communication networks and can work more effectively across distances. But they still need the support of clear decision-making processes, reporting structures, and a variety of reliable tools to aid collaboration and communication.

Building a dense array of communication channels is paramount to the success of a global innovation project. ICTs play an important role in supporting structured communication via video and phone conferences, Web meetings, bulletin boards, and newsletters. But they have to be supplemented by off-site meetings, temporary periods of colocation, and site visits. Without face-to-face communication, teams can't share the embedded and complex knowledge critical to integrating a modular architecture effectively, strengthen trust, or build buddy networks.

For team members coming from a colocated environment, the level and intensity of both formal and informal communication needed in a global project may seem onerous. But they need to understand that communication is an essential part of the workflow, without which they can't flag problems or track progress. In the definition phase, as well as identifying the armory of communication channels required, it is important that scheduling accounts for the time that project teams need to spend on communication.

Throughout the definition phase, there has to be an underlying goal of building consensus between the team members by involving them in the process. A project will proceed much more smoothly when everyone is on the same page. They need to agree on the purpose of the project, how and why it is split over different locations, how different modules interface and what interdependencies exist between them, how reporting structures work, who is responsible for decision making, and what collaboration and communication tools to use. If a company imposes a global project on project teams, they are likely to view it with hostility. After all, global innovation projects can result in longer hours and more work for everyone. But when teams are included in the definition process, they take ownership of the project, their horizons widen, and no challenge is too great to overcome. (See table 6-2 for a summary of the definition phase.)

Delivery: Managing Global Projects

A well-run definition phase should end after achieving buy-in from all team members, a clear breakdown of product architecture, and a capability-based work package division, all of which

TABLE 6-2

The definition phase

What to do	What not to do
• Build a competence for working on global projects (building team capabilities on small projects)	• If your organization is in a state of flux, do not embark on a global project
• Break down project architecture into modules to be divided across sites	• Don't rush the definition phase; defining the project properly takes time
• Clearly specify interfaces and interdependencies before project launch	• Don't skimp on travel and communication costs; periods of temporary colocation will be required
• Share strategic context driving the project with all sites involved	
• Ensure that project sites have complementary competencies with a little overlap	• Don't allocate tasks based on available resources, but on capabilities required

will make the management of the project in the delivery phase more straightforward. But just as the identification and definition phases call for new approaches, so too does the final delivery phase. If a team is going to deliver a successful project built on the groundwork established in the preceding phases, it needs to have clear leadership, heavyweight project management, close senior management involvement, and a limited number of subcontractors.

The Myth of Equal Partners

It's easy to fall into the trap of treating all sites in a global innovation project as equal partners for fear that different innovation sites will resent not being at the top of a hierarchical structure. But a global project is neither a debating society nor a utopian confederation. The idea that all sites involved in the project are equal is nice in theory but untenable in practice. Take the example of Elecompt's Apcantes project. Each site had a high level of autonomy and equal weight in driving the project and decision making based on its own expertise. But collective responsibility failed because the various sites found it difficult to reach a consensus. Each saw the project through the prism of its own background, skills, and context, and no one had oversight to see the big picture.

Global innovation projects need a locus of control, which means assigning one site as the project leader. The lead site then shoulders the responsibility for ensuring that decisions are made and project milestones are reached. The leader also coordinates the integration of the various work packages and manages the transition to production or rollout. In short, it has to deliver the project on time and on budget.

Heavyweight Project Management

The idea of imposing heavyweight management on an innovation project will no doubt elicit the cry that "process stifles creativity." To some extent, we concede, this may be true. But, on the other hand, dispersed creativity that is allowed to flourish unchecked will not deliver any new products or services. Complex projects that are split over multiple boundaries, including time zones, organizations, functions, geographies, and cultures, need the discipline of robust project management structures, tools, and processes.

Heavyweight management of global innovation projects relies on a strong project management organization. When Essilor delivered project Sapphire on time and on budget and, in doing so, introduced an innovative new product to market significantly ahead of its competitors, a strong project management organization played a leading role in its achievement (see sidebar 6-3). Over the many years that Essilor has been running dispersed complex projects, it has built a highly skilled project management organization that garners as much respect within the firm as any of its other innovation-related functions. It is staffed by high-caliber people from a range of functional and national backgrounds. The project managers work closely with senior managers to ensure that budgets and expectations are realistic and that tough decisions are made as fast as possible. They are adaptable individuals who recognize that the complexity of global innovation projects means that standard tools and processes aren't always the best solution for delivering the project and so are able to improvise and adopt alternative approaches when necessary.[5]

Project managers need to travel extensively during the definition and delivery phases of a global project. Organizations that continually deliver successful global projects know this is not an area for budget cutbacks, because a good project management organization is the backbone of a global project.

SIDEBAR 6-3

SAPPHIRE: STRONG PROJECT MANAGEMENT DELIVERING SUCCESS

Transitions Optical is a joint venture between Essilor International, the world's largest ophthalmic lens manufacturer, and U.S. monomer specialist PPG Industries to develop photochromic processes (i.e., enabling lenses to turn dark in sunlight). With customer demands increasing, to retain its leadership position Transitions Optical had to develop a new product from scratch, based on new chemical and manufacturing processes, and get that product to market within eighteen months to stay ahead of its competitors.

The modern eyeglass lens is a highly complex product at the cutting-edge of many technologies. There are up to twenty-six layers of chemical processes embedded within and on a substrate to provide antiscratch, antireflection, antismear, and a whole host of other finishes. Developing the new product required three different sets of competencies. Essilor had deep expertise in lens casting and distribution; PPG's focus was on creating the monomer; and Transitions Optical contributed the expertise in photochromic processing.

The project, Sapphire, involved more than twenty sites worldwide and significant challenges. The new technology had to be applied to multiple products (such as semifinished, single vision, bifocal, multifocal, etc.), each presenting unique manufacturing challenges, and an inventory of a few million lenses had to be built up ahead of the launch.

Essilor, with its strong project management organization, took the lead. A core technology team was set up within Essilor to monitor the development of the various technologies and feed the information back to the dispersed development and production sites. A senior executive from each partner was also assigned to the project in a hands-on role. Despite the short project time frame, the alliance partners invested nine months in working together defining the project and the interfaces between the specialist contributions. For example, they worked to ensure that the monomer could be scaled up, cast, and crafted and that the photochromic dyes could be embedded into the surface of the lens without any adverse reactions from the monomer.

(continued)

Because Essilor's manufacturing sites each specialized in different products requiring unique equipment and processes, there was no blanket solution to scaling up products for production. A team of senior production engineers (all with strong backgrounds in chemistry) joined the project at the outset, working in product development teams. By understanding how the final product had been developed, the production engineers were equipped to set up each unique manufacturing site for production of the new photochromic range.

Due to the size and speed of the project, Sapphire faced a constant fight against outdated information. To overcome this, a series of Web sites (one for the core technology team and one each for the alliance partners) were updated daily and included all the latest decisions, outcomes, and progress. Senior managers at each of the alliance partners received a regular executive summary newsletter for the project.

The Transitions New Generation photochromic range of lenses was launched globally on target, thanks to a stringent, well-defined project management process that was totally aligned with both strategic and operational objectives.

Senior Management Involvement and Commitment

For collaboration across sites to work, senior managers must be committed and visibly involved in the project. They perform two main functions: First, they hold ultimate responsibility for quick decision making, which can have a big impact on project success or failure. At Essilor, a member of the executive team is assigned to each project and is responsible for the outcome. During the Sapphire project, shortcuts in the production validation and evaluation processes were suggested as a solution for keeping the project on track to achieve its launch date. Naturally, managers at the eighteen production sites were reluctant to expose themselves to this risk lest they be blamed for any problems with the finished product. The executive responsible for Sapphire informed the executive committee and they agreed to sanction the proposed shortcuts, assuring the production sites that the risk belonged to the project and not the individual sites.

Second, senior managers diffuse any conflicts that may arise between sites. The potential for misinterpretation greatly increases in global projects, and if left unchecked, miscommunications can quickly snowball into debilitating problems. Senior managers use their experience and authority to resolve potential conflicts before they become serious enough to destabilize the project.

Managing Subcontractors

Faster cycle times, convergence across industries, and ongoing efforts to rationalize businesses around core competencies mean that more companies are subcontracting chunks or modules of projects to external experts to either reduce the project delivery time or access new competencies. Although subcontractors play a valuable role, they bring additional complexity; therefore, limiting their participation reduces the management and coordination burden. In practical terms, this means adhering to the following:

- *Stick with trusted partners.* Just as it makes sense to use tried and tested combinations of internal sites wherever possible to collaborate on large global innovation projects, it also makes sense to use trusted subcontractors. They will have a deep understanding of the development and integration processes and project management organization. The ATV-71 project at Schneider Toshiba Inverter had a number of subcontractors it had worked with previously but, in addition, used a Korean subcontractor for the first time. Not long into the project, problems arose with the new subcontractor, which were only resolved after a decision to move them to France so the French team could monitor and support them. Although necessary, this costly and time-consuming action could have been avoided had the project relied on a trusted partner to develop that module.

- *Think about proximity.* Subcontractors should be near one of the internal project sites, because this will, by default, limit the number of cultures and languages in the project and facilitate collaboration. For example, in the ATV-71 project, the Korean subcontractor wasn't close enough geographically or culturally to Japan allow the Japanese project site to supervise or work closely with them.

- *Avoid fuzzy work definitions.* Subcontractors need to have well-specified work packages. Since they don't have detailed knowledge about existing product families, the strategic rationale driving the project, or customer requirements, and are not fully integrated into the project teams, they will not have the flexibility to experiment and adapt their work in the same way an internal project team does.

- *Give experts oversight.* An internal person who has expertise and understanding in the area in which subcontractors are working should oversee their work. Without this oversight, problems won't be identified until the integration stage, at which point they become costly to rectify.

(See table 6-3 for a summary of the delivery phase.)

TABLE 6-3

The delivery phase

What to do	What not to do
• Establish heavyweight project management	• Don't treat project sites as equal partners; one site must be the leader
• Set up dense, formal and informal communication channels	• Don't use large numbers of subcontractors
• Establish common tasks and processes	• Avoid using subcontractors not located near any of the project sites
• Ensure that senior managers are visible and engaged in the project	
• Use tried and tested subcontractors	

Over the past two decades, the nature of innovation has changed beyond recognition. To compete in this new environment, companies need to be better equipped to respond with an effective approach to global innovation. Global projects provide an activity around which global resources can be marshaled and organized. They impose the tools and processes needed to find and meld knowledge worldwide. And they put in place the structures and systems needed to collaborate over time and distance.

Although the concept of global innovation projects is not new, it hasn't gained many advocates. For those companies that have experimented with global projects, success has been fleeting and, in many cases, elusive. These results shouldn't be interpreted as an indication of what global projects really have to offer. The problems most companies have experienced are due to the fact that they have merely transferred the best practice of colocated projects to an arena in which sites are dispersed. They have overlooked the difficulties inherent in organizing and undertaking complex projects across many boundaries. Global projects are complex and systemic. They require senior management focus and attention and, as such, can only flourish in stable

FIGURE 6-2

Decision tree for structuring and managing global projects

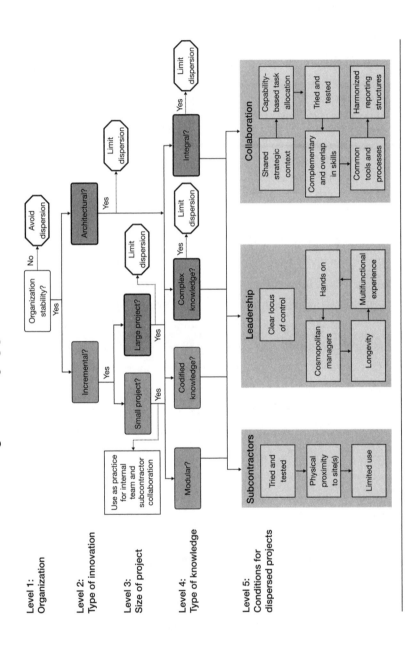

Level 1:
Organization

Level 2:
Type of innovation

Level 3:
Size of project

Level 4:
Type of knowledge

Level 5:
Conditions for
dispersed projects

environments where management isn't preoccupied with other major events. They rely on people with different backgrounds, cultures, norms, languages, and experiences to work together with the added difficulty of multiple time zones.

To be successful, companies have to dismantle the preconceptions and prejudices caused by these differences. When they distribute work across multiple locations, communication dwindles and withers away. But good-quality communication is a cornerstone of global projects. The complexity and scale of global projects precludes anything being left to chance. Whereas, in colocated projects, work can start and the product architecture, interfaces, or functionality can be adapted as the project progresses, in global innovation projects, the company needs to think through and plan for every eventuality at the drawing board. Figure 6-2 presents the main dangers, conditions, and decisions that a company needs to consider in managing global projects.

We don't pretend that global innovation projects are as easy to set up, run, and manage as colocated ones, just as we don't claim that colocated projects can deliver the same benefits as their global counterparts. But, by following the three-stage process of identification, definition, and delivery, the outcome of global projects needn't be serendipitous. Instead, companies that employ this process will be able to leverage their global footprint with a powerful competence that equips them to deliver a pipeline of unique innovations that build competitive advantage.

CHAPTER SEVEN

Collaborative Innovation

F or many companies, global projects inevitably become a necessity simply because of the growing need for collaborative innovation. But the idea of collaboration is much more than offshoring or bringing in subcontractors to develop specific modules, which we discussed in the previous chapter. As we have stressed throughout this book, the knowledge a company needs for innovation is increasingly dispersed not only geographically but across different sectors and specialties. So a company will find some of the critical knowledge, skills, and capabilities needed for innovation in other firms.

Attracting, foraying, and experiencing are the constituents of an agile footprint, as we discussed in chapter 2. But we cautioned that experiencing to access complex, locally rooted knowledge was difficult and costly, and the risk of failure was potentially high. In some scenarios, however, there is an alternative to experiencing: firms should consider whether they really need a local presence or a local partner in order to access knowledge. Collaborating with the holders of knowledge, particularly when that knowledge is very different from a company's own areas of competence, is a logical step in accessing and creating value from that knowledge.

The nature of collaboration is likely to vary and evolve over the course of an innovation project; we use the same framework for thinking about the different stages of collaborative projects as in the previous chapter (see figure 7-1). But there is one difference: the framework for an in-house global project doesn't include the diffusion stage of the innovation because channels familiar to the firm can usually handle diffusion. In collaborative

FIGURE 7-1

Changing shape of a collaborative innovation project

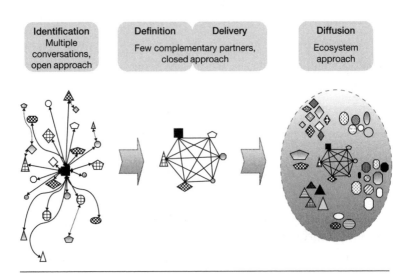

Identification	Definition	Delivery	Diffusion
Multiple conversations, open approach	Few complementary partners, closed approach		Ecosystem approach

scenarios, however, diffusing an innovation presents some challenges that call for new skills and capabilities. Therefore, we have added a distinct diffusion phase to the innovation project framework.

In this chapter, we explore the nature of the collaboration required at the identification, definition, delivery, and diffusion stages of an innovation project. During the identification phase of a collaborative innovation, it's important to cast the net wide. In the context of innovation through knowledge combination, the ideas for an innovative new product or service will often result from a wide network of contributors bringing together aspects of potentially unmet customer needs, new technologies, and other seemingly disparate elements of knowledge. Open mind-sets and mechanisms that enable a firm to capture many inputs to discover, sharpen, and shape the innovation opportunity are suitable at this early stage.

The definition and delivery phases of a project require complementary and cospecialized contributions; therefore a tight, structured approach involving few partners is more effective. The collaborative development of an innovation means identifying the various partners that can bring unique capabilities and skills and marshaling them around well-defined tasks. But, integrating the contributions is difficult and complex (more so than in the global projects described in chapter 6) because each partner may bring very different knowledge to the project, with little overlap between contributions—a challenge that increases with the number of partners involved.

In the final phase, the diffusion of an innovation, a broader collaborative approach may be needed again. The success of an innovation in the market often relies on a range of stakeholders providing complementary goods. As in the identification phase, an open but regulated and structured process involving many participants accelerates the diffusion of an innovation.

Collaborative Identification

For the best ideas to surface and develop, the identification phase in collaborative projects has to be open and exploratory. Achieving this calls for action on three fronts. First, opening and maintaining dialogues to explore new ideas. Second, engaging in open innovation activities to build on and test those embryonic ideas. And finally, choosing the right partners to bring maximum advantage to the identification stage.

Opening and Building on Conversations

Collaboration can significantly contribute to the identification of innovation opportunities. After all, innovative ideas do not originate in a vacuum but more often result from new conversations, whether intentional or serendipitous. We saw earlier how Novartis opened an innovation hub in the United States near MIT in order to foster and facilitate exactly these sorts of conversations. And it isn't alone; many companies pursue similar strategies to colocate some of their innovation activities with leading universities and research institutes.

Ideas for innovations rarely surface fully formed but emerge as fragments of an idea that need nurturing, developing, and aligning with other complementary fragments. Multiple conversations with people outside a company's boundaries not only create the opportunity for new innovations to be conceived, but provide a breeding ground for those ideas to then be scrutinized, improved on, or superseded. A hallmark of successful innovators is their ability to rapidly sharpen, test, reconsider, and reshape innovation ideas as their understanding deepens. A wide network of collaboration partners emulates the successful innovator, because by engaging in the conversation about an innovative idea, a company can explore various business models and technologies and the initial idea rapidly evolves into something more concrete and workable.

The Role of Open Innovation

In a world of dispersed knowledge, a company can collaborate to extend and leverage its ability to access new knowledge once initial conversations have revealed interesting new opportunities for further exploration. The broad range of collective innovation phenomena that fall under the heading of open innovation provides the ideal medium to do this. A more open innovation approach should provide a good understanding of the latent needs the innovation might serve in different or unfamiliar markets and alert the company to the opportunities, technologies, and knowledge that it can bring into the innovation. The wider the collaboration at this point, the greater the likelihood robust solutions to problems will arise or new ideas will match emerging needs.

Additionally, a more open collaboration approach is better suited to complex problems that have systemic solutions. Many IT companies, for instance, see a growing opportunity in applying advanced technology to complex and systemic societal problems, such as health care and efficient energy production.

The identification of this type of innovation needs to be open and embrace a wide range of experts in different fields.

Choosing Partners for the Identification Phase

A range of considerations should drive the choice of partners in the identification stage of an innovation project (see figure 7-2).

Maximize Diversity

The whole point of collaboration is to elicit new and, diverse knowledge. While a company may be tempted and find it less difficult to seek knowledge that is close to home, partners provide a different perspective and opportunity for reframing rather than merely confirming orthodoxies and assumptions. In other

FIGURE 7-2

Partner selection criteria for collaborative innovation

Identification	Definition and Delivery	Diffusion
Look to: • Maximize diversity to promote reframing and different perspectives • Access extended networks through partners • Opportunities for reciprocal learning • Seek the best and brightest for optimal breadth and depth • Focus on value-creation opportunities for all, not value capture for one partner • Ensure partners have compatible levels of commitment	Ensure partners: • Possess the right capabilities that are up to speed for the project • Cospecialized with complementary capabilities, not duplication • Equal contributions and rights in relation to existing IP or assets brought to project • Understand motives and degree of commitment • Reputation and credibility as good partners • Culturally compatible (management style, size) • Share strategic ambitions	Ecosystem requires: • Catalyst to build ecosystem • Rallying around a cause • Symbiotic relationship between partners • Identification of as many interdependencies as possible and partners found • Identification of critical partners and choke points • Cultural compatibility and shared norms for problem solving • Transparent collective value creation proposition • Clear understanding of mutual benefits

words, it's vital to seek variety and maximize the diversity of inputs, analytical perspectives, and creative insights.

Access Extended Networks

Beyond what they themselves can contribute, partners should be able and willing to provide access to other potential partners from their own networks. In network theory terms, the breadth and scope offered by many weak ties is preferable to few strong ties. The Moscow Aviation Institute we referred to in chapter 2, for instance, offered that opportunity to Snecma during its identification of Russian space-propulsion plasma technologies. Of course, not all identification-stage partners bring useful contributions, insightful ideas, or novel perspectives. But some may have access to extended networks that can yield critical knowledge to the innovation.

Learn with Partners

During the process of collaboration, the knowledge and experience each partner contributes should complement a firm's core knowledge base and provide the foundation for reciprocal learning. Good learning partners may not be industry leaders or laggards. But they will be eager to use the collaboration to improve their own market and competitive positions, and willing to invest the required resources in the identification phase and potentially in the subsequent phases. IBM's approach to its "collaboratories" is an interesting example of collaborating with learning partners (see sidebar 7-1). IBM works with a range of local partners, each of which provides complementary knowledge and experience that enables everyone in the collaboration to engage in joint and individual learning.

SIDEBAR 7-1

IBM'S COLLABORATORIES

The world is our lab now ... I can have a much larger impact on the
company and our research if I operate that way.

—John E. Kelly III, IBM director of research

IBM, no neophyte to internationalization, has long had research
centers in Switzerland, Japan, Israel, and the United Kingdom, and
more recently opened labs in China and India. These labs draw on
local capabilities and talent and link with local research institutes
like ETH Zürich, the Polytechnic Institute in Switzerland, and
Technion, the leading technical research university in Israel.

IBM decided to extend its global footprint to create a series of
collaborative venture labs ("collaboratories," in IBM parlance). IBM
and its local partners—universities, government institutes, and
companies—cocreate, costaff, and cofund the labs. They have
established collaboratories in China, India, Ireland, Saudi Arabia,
Switzerland, and Taiwan, all with different mandates.

Some of the collaboratories focus on technologies that can
deliver short-term results and fit within IBM's Smart Planet
initiative—a plan to develop solutions that address, both locally and
globally, environmental and societal issues, such as electric power
grid optimization and transport systems. Others have grand, long-
term aims; for example, the joint semiconductor lab with ETH Zürich
for nanotechnologies. Here, the goal is to research entirely new
microelectronics switching technologies that might replace existing
semiconductors, once the density and thinness of integrated
circuits reach the physical limits of conductivity.

There are also more market-oriented collaboratories. For instance, in 2008, IBM started working with China Telecom to apply advanced data analysis methodologies and computing power to analyze China Telecom's huge database of client information. China Telecom wanted to better understand customer needs from its vast quantity of data and craft better offers, packages, terms, and conditions for integrated fixed-line, mobile, and broadband data services. Accessing the China Telecom data gave IBM the opportunity to try out new technologies and data analysis algorithms on huge amounts of real-life data. IBM has applied some of the findings from this collaboration to the services it provides to other telecom companies.

A point of commonality across the collaboratories is that they work on significant breakthrough opportunities where skills and knowledge are needed from both IBM and the local partners for innovation. In addition, the collaboratories create value for IBM and the local partner(s) beyond the purely local benefits. Although the interests of each party are different, they are congruent. Of course, there are some difficult issues of ownership of intellectual property rights (IPR) and, more generally, value capture (in particular, with universities that may be subject to government funding and IPR ownership rules). These issues have occasionally made collaboration impossible, but in the vast majority of cases, shared interests and objectives have overcome such differences.

Seek Depth and Breadth

The identification phase comprises largely intellectual and creative inputs. Simple as it may sound, bright partners bring more to the table. A mix of depth in specific areas and breadth in ability to connect these areas to others is a valuable trait in partners. Yet, to an extent, the complex marketplace for collaboration, in which a firm's reputation for innovation and its history for being a good partner, removes some degree of choice when identifying partners for collaboration. For example, highly innovative German-based car electronics companies were unwilling to collaborate with the European operations of General Motors. From their perspective, General Motors lagged in technological innovation and was reluctant to invest seriously in collaborative innovation. The fact that the German companies chose to collaborate with automakers like BMW, Daimler-Benz, and Volkswagen was not because of techno-nationalism, but just their recognition that they could learn more from and with them than with General Motors. In short, they saw General Motors as lacking the depth and breadth to make a valuable contribution to co-innovation.

Focus on Value Creation

Potential partners are unlikely to invest wholeheartedly in collaboration at the identification phase unless they sense that the resulting innovations will benefit them in some way. But while a focus on value creation is essential, there is a danger that some firms, in particular industry leaders, may exhibit a natural propensity for value capture. An overemphasis on "what's in it for me?" at this stage risks restricting the innovation opportunity, making it difficult to explore the full potential of an innovative idea and maintain an identification phase mind-set. Of course, the partners in a collaboration can't ignore the issue of how to share the benefits from the innovation, but this consideration should be secondary, only after the full potential of the innovation has been scoped out.

Intel Labs Europe is a good example of collaboration focusing on value creation, not on value capture. In 2009, Intel launched the initiative, with the mission to advance its own architecture research and innovation, while at the same time improving elements of European competitiveness and society. Intel established a number of open labs in Europe, each collaborating with leading local partners. In France, for example, a project called Exascale, focusing on the development and optimization of hugely powerful computers (those with over one billion operations per second), involved collaboration with the nuclear energy commissariat, a national giant computer lab, and the University of Versailles. There were clear value-creation benefits for everyone involved. The local partners saw Exascale as a key tool in supporting France's and Europe's research in nuclear energy and other computation-intensive areas. It also contributed to the advancement of digital health and digital education. For Intel, the value-creation opportunity was in being able to develop supercomputers that would enable it to leapfrog the competition.

Align Commitment

The ideal partners for collaborating in the identification (and later stages, of course) of innovative opportunities are those that share a similar level of commitment to the project. Aligning commitments is extremely difficult: different partners will have varying strategic objectives that can affect the importance they place on an opportunity. As we already mentioned, some partners may focus more on value capture than on committing to the process of collaborative innovation. Or, in cross-industry projects, the challenges in one domain may be significantly greater than in others, requiring too great a commitment.

For example, when mobile phones began to incorporate radio receivers, Nokia came up with the idea of the "visual radio," in which information relevant to the broadcast could be displayed on the screen. Its lead partner in the identification of this innovation was HP, which had a digital broadcasting systems business. The levels of commitment were very different between the partners. For Nokia, the innovation was relatively simple, requiring the addition of a few features to a radio chip. For HP, it was a much more challenging proposition: it saw the innovation in terms of an extremely complex business model with advertisers providing content and paying commissions on sales generated, radio stations adopting the service (these were not a homogeneous customer set), and telecom operators billing purchases made by listeners. From HP's perspective, collaborating on visual radio would require development, testing, and experimentation that involved many different ecosystem players. The project required a level of commitment that was too high for HP, which pulled out of the partnership, to be replaced by a media and advertising firm.

Collaborative Definition and Delivery

The far-reaching, open approach of the identification phase is seldom appropriate in the definition and delivery phase. As the collaboration moves from exploring opportunities and articulating ideas to actually developing an innovation, the number of partners involved reduces and the nature of the collaboration changes from being open to closed. There are several straightforward reasons for this. First, during the definition and delivery of the innovation, both the need for competitive secrecy and the value of the intellectual property (IP) increase dramatically. To protect the newly created IP, projects need to be confidential.

Second, the sheer complexity involved in managing dispersed collaborative projects points to the advantage of having fewer partners. As time to market is critical and many innovations require the simultaneous availability of various components and contributions, the more partners involved—each with their own pressures and priorities—the greater the risk of missing deadlines. For example, the development of the Boeing 787 Dreamliner suffered from having too many risk-bearing partners (see sidebar 7-2). The management of the overall project proved difficult, and the complexity involved in coordinating and integrating the various contributions of the partners led to significant delays.

SIDEBAR 7-2

BOEING: FROM DREAMLINER TO NIGHTMARE PROJECT

When the project was launched, Boeing's 787 Dreamliner was billed not only as a breakthrough aircraft but also as a highly innovative development and manufacturing partnership. While Boeing retained control of the overall plane architecture, each subsection was developed by separate partners, including six in Japan, six in Britain, five in France, two each in Germany and Sweden, one each in South Korea and Italy, in addition to a number of companies in the United States.

In this type of development, partners are usually brought in at the delivery stage. For the Dreamliner, Boeing tapped into the expertise of its partners in the definition phase. The reason for this was that, to improve fuel economy and reduce operating costs considerably,

(continued)

Boeing wanted to make the structure of the Dreamliner from innovative composite materials, and the advanced competencies required to work with composite materials resided with some of the partner companies, such as Mitsubishi, not Boeing.

The ambition and scale of the project soon began to present problems. Boeing had relatively little insight into what was happening at each of its partners. The project was undermanaged, which meant that keeping track of the work at the various locations was more difficult than anticipated. Boeing had not defined the overall architecture and interfaces between major sections with sufficient precision to allow a smooth transition from development to manufacturing. The assembly of major composite material components was also an issue, because the fasteners and handling technologies for large structural components had to be developed before the exact specifications for the interfaces were clear; this resulted in major problems relating to the wing's attachment to the fuselage. As the project progressed, with constituent parts coming together, Boeing had to make extensive modifications, adding considerable weight to the plane and negating some of its expected fuel-efficiency benefits.

Boeing resorted to temporary colocation. For over six months in 2005, teams from the various partners worked together at Boeing to jointly redefine the configuration of the plane, work that Boeing had previously always done on its own. Between configuration and production, the various partners undertook detailed parts development in six weekly meetings and frequent video conferencing.

In September 2007, eight months before the first deliveries were due, Boeing announced the first of five delays to delivery dates. The 787 finally made its maiden flight in December 2009, with the first plane being delivered in the fall of 2011. These delays caused Boeing enormous embarrassment, particularly as the new plane was a commercial success. Boeing had received around nine hundred orders even before the 787's first flight. The delays also meant the competitive lead Boeing had enjoyed was considerably eroded, as the competing Airbus A350 picked up orders. In addition, Boeing saw its share price halved, as doubts about the timing and success of the Dreamliner project began to emerge.

By shifting to collaborative global innovation involving over fifty main partners and at the same time pioneering new composite material technologies and putting in place new program management tools, Boeing had compounded its difficulties. It combined technical, organizational, and managerial innovations with unprecedented ambitions.

Finally, when entering a collaboration with innovation partners, a company needs to clearly understand the motives driving each partner. Although all partners don't necessarily need exactly the same objectives, they do need to be compatible and congruent. Otherwise, there is a significant risk that each measures success differently, which makes collaboration difficult. The fewer the partners, the easier it is to ensure that motives align and the benefits of the innovation accrue jointly between the partners and not disproportionately to any individual partner. A clearer understanding of motives also protects the innovation from free riders.

Selecting Partners for Definition and Delivery

Selecting the right partners for the tightly knit definition and delivery phases of an innovation project is absolutely critical.

There are seven key dimensions to choosing partners, which, if met, will not only bring the best combination of knowledge and competencies to the project but also help overcome some of the cultural differences that could hamper the management of the project and eventually derail the collaboration (see the definition and delivery section in figure 7-2).

Accurate Capability Assessment

When involved in the excitement of negotiating a collaborative innovation project, potential partners in good faith can get carried away with the momentum of the opportunity and overstate or overestimate their capabilities. But a foundation of optimism, no matter how sincere, instead of realism is not a good basis for collaborative definition and delivery. Each partner needs to have the proven competencies, capabilities, and skills to meet its commitments. Any shortfall in contributions not only will result in costly delays to the project but could prove fatal to the success of the innovation.

Complementarity and Cospecialization

Capabilities obviously need to be highly complementary and cospecialized so each acquires value only when combined with the others. Partners should not use the collaboration as an experiment or a pretext to learn for their own benefit. Whatever interpartner rivalry or competition may exist, everyone involved needs to commit to shared success by making the best possible contribution and providing the most unique, differentiating capabilities. Interpartner negotiations on value capture can then focus on the valuation of the unique cospecialized contributions. The more unique the various contributions are, the more equal the value each partner will bring to the collaboration.

Contribution Assessment

In collaborations that create a common entity from, say, a patent pool or a tool library, some partners may be tempted to keep their most valuable assets, patents, research teams, customer relationships, or supplier agreements to themselves. Agreements and assurances must cover intellectual property rights, contributions, and the conditions of access to capabilities that partners do not bring into the collaboration but make available to it.

Partners' Motives and Commitment

As we suggested earlier, different partners have different motives for collaborating in an innovation project; these drive their commitment to the project. Too great a divergence in motives and commitment puts the project at high risk of never reaching its goals, because some partners don't share the same sense of timing and urgency and some may simply lose interest. Particularly in rapidly evolving domains, the collaborative project may be just an option that quickly outlives its usefulness for some, while being a lifeline for others.

Understanding the motives and gaining the commitment of large companies in collaborative projects can be particularly difficult. For large partners, the innovation alliance can be held hostage to a wider set of strategic considerations that may end an otherwise healthy collaboration. Take the example of PixTech's alliance (see sidebar 7-3). One of the key partners divested the division that had been working on the collaboration, and the new owner wasn't interested in continuing the project. Other large partners viewed the collaboration as an insurance policy while they pursued alternatives. Without aligned motives and equal levels of commitment to the end goal, what began as a promising project to develop a superior product ground to a halt. To understand the importance of a particular alliance to a partner's activities is not simple, yet it is essential to the success of collaborative innovation projects.

SIDEBAR 7-3

PIXTECH: FROM GREAT POTENTIAL TO DOWNFALL

PixTech was founded by a French entrepreneur, Jean-Luc Grand Clément. In the Grenoble microelectronics lab of the French nuclear energy commissariat, he spotted an idea for an interesting innovation: a new type of flat-panel display that he thought had the potential to overcome many of the limitations of liquid crystal display (LCD) and plasma screens.

PixTech developed a strategy whereby, sequenced over time, a series of partners would develop a string of applications, starting with simple, small-screen black-and-white devices and moving to complex, demanding ones. The same partners would also contribute complementary competencies to allow PixTech's technologies to compete with those of industry leaders.

But PixTech did not pay enough attention to the risks of losing partners or of partners with different motivations and commitments to the project. One of its first partners was Texas Instruments' personal computer division. Even though the collaboration went well relatively early on, corporate management at Texas Instruments decided to exit from personal computers and sold the division to Acer. Acer had little appetite for exploring a new screen technology, so PixTech lost a critical partner. Another partner, Motorola, was interested in high-quality screens for mobile phones. But, to

---

Motorola, PixTech's technology was insurance against the failure of alternative, cheaper technologies, such as LCDs. Other large, mass-market partners in the collaboration took stances similar to Motorola's. Eventually, PixTech found its project restricted to narrow, small-volume, niche applications in medical monitoring and avionics.

Even with the diffusion of the scaled-down innovation, PixTech overestimated the commitment of its manufacturing partner, United Microelectronics. The bread-and-butter of its business was the manufacture of LCDs for demanding, high-quality applications, and the company turned out to be less than enthused about the prospect of cannibalizing its own business. When it came to manufacturing, ramping up, and solving problems related to PixTech's products, United Microelectronics dragged its feet. In the end, PixTech went bankrupt and was taken over by Micron, an associate of Intel. Its technology—although superior to alternatives, in principle—remained marginal in the world of flat-panel displays.

Credibility as Good Partners

We discussed in the previous chapter the importance of experience and trust in global projects. When the project is collaborative, the reputation of a company as a good partner is crucial. When firms haven't worked together before, reputation and credibility indicate how well each works in collaboration. However, although a potential partner with no credibility for collaborative innovation may be an issue, selecting partners based on strong credibility alone doesn't guarantee success. High levels of credibility or previous experience and familiarity in innovating together may lead partners to rely excessively on trust and overlook potential strategic weaknesses underlying the collaboration or its design. While credibility is important, it cannot override all the other dimensions in choosing a partner.

Cultural Compatibility

Companies should not see cultural incompatibility as an insurmountable barrier to collaboration. But they should be aware of the issues that different cultures bring to a project and, based on its scope and scale, decide whether managing these differences will be too difficult.

One divisive cultural difference facing collaborations is the various partners' speed of decision making and work pace. Another difference is the discrepancy in autonomy within a hierarchy. For example, companies from countries with strong hierarchical management structures (common in Latin countries, for example) are less likely to delegate responsibility than those with flat management structures (typical in Scandinavian firms), making collaboration frustrating.

The size of partners also affects cultural compatibility. Small firms tend to be entrepreneurial and agile, while their large counterparts are, on the whole, slow and bureaucratic. The small firm shouldn't have to adopt more procedural innovation management, which its own management will deeply resent. If a large partner knows it can't make this adjustment, it should reconsider collaborations with small, innovative firms.

If cultural differences remain the only stumbling block to partner selection, the project may overcome incompatibility by establishing a separate autonomous entity to interface between partners and buffer direct contacts between them. However, some socialization between the team members of each partner is important, and this could influence partner selection. Our survey found that when collaborating on innovation projects, firms usually chose partners located close to their own innovation centers. Proximity with external partners not only facilitates informal communication, but reduces some cultural differences.

Compatible Strategic Ambitions

A viable collaboration can happen only if the partners have shared strategic ambitions for what they want the project to achieve and compatible objectives for what they want to gain from the collaboration. A good example of the impact of compatible strategic ambitions is the Airbus consortium. Despite political and social vicissitudes, this collaboration has been remarkably stable over decades because the goals of each partner align. The long-term success of Airbus is based on the principle of complementarity and cospecialization, with no encroachment of skills between partners. For example, British Aerospace is responsible for wing design and manufacture, which enables it to hone its competencies and continually challenge a critical mass of engineers. Not only does the Airbus consortium get the best wings for its planes, but British Aerospace is able to maintain a lead as one of the world's best wing designers.

Conversely, when some of the same partners from the successful Airbus consortium came together to develop the military Typhoon fighter plane, their strategic ambitions and objectives did not align. They ignored the principle of cospecialization, and none were willing to relinquish the full range of competencies required to develop the plane. Worse still, all were eager to learn from their partners' skills, which resulted in technology leaks and suspicion among the partners, leading to contentious, costly, and ineffective programs. Divergence in the partners' strategic objectives was eventually overcome only when European governments exerted pressure.

To summarize, when moving to the codefinition and delivery of an innovation, fewer partners should be involved, so companies must pay careful attention to their selection. Awareness of potential areas of conflict, misalignment, or problems enables the collaboration partners to assess and reduce many potential difficulties through project design, structure, and management. However, one area remains an exception: strategic incompatibility among the partners' objectives poses an intractable barrier to collaboration during the definition and delivery of an innovation.

Collaborative Diffusion

Beyond identification, definition, and delivery, innovations also need diffusion and distribution partners, or independent companies that play a mutually supportive role. Without complementary partners at this stage, the innovation will not succeed commercially but will remain an interesting experiment. A classic example of the symbiotic relationship at the diffusion stage is JVC and Matsushita's development of the VHS standard video player, the emergent video home-rental industry, and, in particular, the growth of large movie rental chains like Blockbuster. Companies like Netflix and LOVEFiLM have extended that logic to home movie streaming; as Internet providers and cable companies provide increased broadband speeds, movies can be digitally encoded, and processor capacities can increasingly support vast quantities of data.

In some cases, the diffusion of an innovation necessitates building an ecosystem. But it is important not to move to ecosystem building too quickly. For innovations that are incremental and/or elemental, ecosystems probably already exist to aid the diffusion. For example, when Bosch created a new high-pressure direct-injection fuel pump, carmakers were eagerly awaiting the new product and regulators were calling for it. But accessing an existing ecosystem to promote the diffusion of a next-generation innovation may prove difficult if it is located in unfamiliar or distant markets. Despite the challenges, finding and tapping into a compatible existing ecosystem is almost always preferable to and easier than trying to build a new one.

Existing ecosystems for the diffusion of an innovation won't always welcome the arrival of a new innovation because it proves to be disruptive and challenges vested interests. Take, for example, the slow adoption of credit cards with embedded chips. Although these so-called smart cards use a customer's personal identification number (PIN) to make fraud more difficult, banks, particularly in the United States, were reluctant to adopt and roll out the new technology. They had huge investments in magnetic-strip cards and did not want or could not afford to migrate to the innovative, safer, smart cards. Here, the disruption to the diffusion ecosystem (the banks) meant it took years to get the innovation to market.

Building Distributed Innovation Ecosystems

When a diffusion ecosystem doesn't already exist because the innovation is radical and architectural, then the company must create a new ecosystem. The process of building a new ecosystem begins early in the innovation process. But only firms with deep pockets and strong competencies have adequate resources. First, they have to define a cause around which they can rally the ecosystem players. Next, they have to help key players see how supporting the cause will result in collective value creation. And, finally, they need to create forums that will promote the ecosystem and the innovation. Over the course of a decade, Intel created a global ecosystem to promote the diffusion of a new 4G wireless broadband technology, WiMAX (see sidebar 7-4).[1] It brought in a wide array of global partners to establish an infrastructure and enable WiMAX to get to market ahead of competing 4G services.

SIDEBAR 7-4

INTEL: BUILDING THE WIMAX INNOVATION ECOSYSTEM

By the early 2000s, Intel's strategists recognized that wired broadband wasn't going to provide enough stimulus to increase sales of laptops, desktops, and, hence, Intel processors. The cost of taking fiber optics into homes proved a barrier to growth, so Intel began looking for solutions to overcome that hurdle. Wireless broadband seemed the obvious answer and, in particular, a new technology—worldwide interoperability for microwave access (WiMAX).

One Intel division had already been involved in developing the standard for a long-range, wireless, commercial-grade network, IEEE 802.16. Intel could continue to work on developing the industry standard, or it could have chosen the faster route of developing its own proprietary chip. Because WiMAX had to be an ecosystem innovation (Intel would only be a component supplier to the technology), Intel chose the industry standard route. Initially, only a handful of other companies worked on the 802.16, but as the ecosystem grew, the snowball effect took hold and hundreds of firms became involved.

Before Intel could embed WiMAX capabilities in its chips for fixed devices and laptops, it had to have an infrastructure in place to support the new technology. So, in parallel with the development of a WiMAX chipset, Intel had to build a wider WiMAX innovation ecosystem. In 2002, it acquired a high-tech start-up that had developed wireless broadband equipment. At the same time, Intel brought component suppliers, infrastructure suppliers, and end-user device manufacturers into the ecosystem. WiMAX offered them a range of next-generation benefits, from seamless networking to reduced power consumption.

During the next year, Intel realized that, although it had framed the WiMAX opportunity in terms of an alternative to fixed-line broadband and WiFi, it had overlooked the huge potential in the mobile telecom market. In mid-2003, Intel decided to expand the WiMAX proposition into the 4G telecom space, which presented new challenges: the infrastructure investment and development required would be huge, and mobile operators would have to choose to adopt WiMAX as the next-generation technology. After making significant investments in 3G technologies, many were reluctant to commit to 4G alternatives. Even if they did commit, WiMAX would face stiff competition from the alternative long-term evolution (LTE) technology, which AT&T and Verizon were rumored to be backing.

In Intel's favor, the development of WiMAX was around two years ahead of the competition, but to maintain this lead would require an enlarged ecosystem. Intel brought equipment manufacturers, including Dell, HTC, LG, Motorola, Samsung, Sony, and Toshiba, into the ecosystem, because they agreed to put the WiMAX technology in their devices. Samsung had been working on its own standard in Korea, but decided to converge it with the

(*continued*)

802.16 range of standards for greater global coverage. WiMAX base stations had to be developed and deployed, so infrastructure suppliers including Alcatel-Lucent, Fujitsu, Huawei, and Siemens joined the ecosystem. Intel brought in core network suppliers, including Cisco and Juniper Networks, and a number of equipment testing and measurement specialists.

As the ecosystem innovation gained momentum, content owners such as Time Warner and Google also joined because they were interested in finding fast ways of delivering multimedia content to their customers. Similarly, a number of cable companies joined because they wanted to add wireless services to their fixed-line broadband, telephone, and television bundles.

By 2006, the WiMAX ecosystem Intel had built still lacked a critical partner—a major mobile telecom operator. In 2004, Intel had invested $20 million in a young mobile operator, Clearwire, which had unused spectrum outside the United States and had agreed to adopt WiMAX. This investment gave the ecosystem a fallback position if a major operator didn't commit to WiMAX. Early on, Intel had identified Sprint as a potential partner because it had unused spectrum in the United States that would be ideal for a WiMAX service. But Sprint was still investigating other alternatives. Without a large operator, Clearwire was the only option, but it simply wasn't big enough to invest in the building of a nationwide network. With Sprint still undecided, in July 2006, Intel and Motorola invested $900 million in Clearwire to put it in a position where it could deploy WiMAX more widely.

A month later, Sprint announced that it had decided to adopt WiMAX for its 4G network and invest $5.5 billion in building a nationwide network over the next two years. Sprint's choice to join the WiMAX camp was due to the fact that Intel had built a strong ecosystem around the technology that would enable it to launch 4G ahead of its competitors.

By the end of the decade, WiMAX had been rolled out around the world and was still expanding. Intel was no longer the primary driver of WiMAX development and deployment; a number of other large companies had made serious investments in the ecosystem. However, Intel had recognized that it needed an ecosystem for the diffusion of its WiMAX chipset innovation, leading to a truly global innovation.

Managing the growth of an innovation ecosystem requires specific skills and the ability to analyze, think, and plan systemically. As the WiMAX story illustrates, over time, an ecosystem is likely to grow in complexity as more complementary contributions are required. This complexity has to be managed so that new opportunities are picked up, potential problems spotted, and the ecosystem players continue to work toward the same goals.

Being a Catalyst for Collaboration

For an innovation ecosystem to be built, some entity, either private or public, has to take the lead. Although building an ecosystem is a complex process, individual innovations may not be feasible without one. That people all over the world are now using WiMAX 4G technology was made possible only because Intel was willing to initiate the ecosystem and rally other companies to the cause.

Leading the Ecosystem

The company or set of companies initiating an innovation ecosystem have an early choice to make. Do they have the time, skills, and resources to lead the ecosystem? Or is their role that of a broker, delegating the management of the ecosystem to a neutral third party?

Understanding the Potential Interdependencies

To ensure the ecosystem is engaged with all relevant groups of players, companies need to appreciate the interdependencies between various stakeholders and the benefits that may accrue. In new and emerging industries, these interdependencies are often far from obvious. Take electric cars as an example. The true pollution impact of electric cars depends on how the electricity is produced and how the batteries are recycled. If a breakthrough development occurred in battery technology, opening the way for long-range electric cars, then electricity production to fuel the batteries would become an issue. Involving energy producers early in the ecosystem conversations would be useful, even though their contribution would come much later.

Identifying the Critical Partners and Choke Points

The sequence in which partners are brought into the ecosystem has an impact on its success, as all the various contributors need to come into play, but not necessarily at the same point. While everyone plays a valuable role in the ecosystem, the lack of a critical type of partner to the diffusion of the innovation will create a choke point. In the WiMAX case, the choke point was a major mobile operator. Ascertaining where the choke point is and finding a suitable partner to fulfill that role early in the innovation process provides stability to the ecosystem and helps the innovation reach its target market on time.

Developing Shared Norms for Problem Solving

Unless the diffusion partners can solve problems collaboratively, the alliance may be short-lived and the innovation may never take off. Our earlier discussion on the issues of cultural compatibility in partner selection for the definition and delivery stage is also relevant here to some extent. But diffusion ecosystems, by their very nature, tend to be large, comprising partners from different industries and fields, so particular effort has to be made to understand how the various partners usually operate. Inclusive forums and working groups become the vehicles for ecosystem debate and problem solving.

Developing and Evangelizing the Mutual Benefits

The benefits of an innovation that come purely from collaboration in the ecosystem and are not achievable by working alone need to be stressed. Visionary insight about the potential of the innovation is the key here, along with a keen sense of how the innovation can play to the interests of each ecosystem partner. In the case of radical innovations that take some firms out of their comfort zones, an emphasis on the compatibility of the innovation with their existing business is an important message to convey.

Collaborative innovation can bring significant benefits at every stage of the innovation process. It opens up a raft of new ideas and opportunities to explore. It provides a vehicle for innovating by combining different and distant knowledge, but in an environment where the risk is shared. And it enables complex innovations to reach global markets in a relatively short time. However, it is also fraught with difficulties. Being aware of the challenges that collaborative innovation poses, can, for the most part, arm companies to build the decision-making processes and management mechanisms to overcome them. There is one barrier, however, that is consistent during the identification, definition, delivery, and diffusion stages of the process, which is more difficult to overcome, simply because it challenges the behavior of decision makers: most senior managers are used to being successful by competing. The genuine change in mind-set and behavior that senior managers need for collaborative innovation is difficult to adopt and sustain. Like all aspects of change, this will only be achieved through practice and positive reinforcement from successful collaborations.

CHAPTER EIGHT

Globally Integrated Innovation

H ow firms innovate needs to change. The increasing
diversity and dispersion of knowledge, the growth of new
markets, and the emergence of new competitors require
a global and integrated approach to innovation. Many executives and managers know that the way their firms currently
organize and carry out innovation has a limited shelf life. But
our research has shown that, despite recognizing the challenge
and being aware that their companies are ill-equipped to meet
it, very few have strategies in place to transform their firms into
global innovators.

In the preceding chapters, we have presented the main challenges to global innovation and put forward a set of frameworks,
tools, and mechanisms to overcome those hurdles and build
an effective, globally integrated innovation capability along
the three dimensions of optimizing the footprint, optimizing
communication and receptivity, and optimizing collaboration

(see figure 8-1). We acknowledge that implementing the necessary changes will take time and determination, as they affect the structure of the innovation organization, systems, processes, culture, mind-sets, and even recruitment and career planning policies. However, it's important that the scope and scale of the task shouldn't become an impediment to action. The nature of the transformation means that change within the three dimensions doesn't have to take place in parallel. In fact, the successful implementation of an element of change in one dimension will have a positive impact on other areas due to the systemic nature of innovation activities.

With this in mind, rather than use this chapter to summarize our findings and suggestions, we propose an action plan based on the three dimensions of change. This plan doesn't represent an exhaustive list of what a company needs to do during the process of building the structures and capabilities for globally integrated

FIGURE 8-1

Building a globally integrated innovation capability

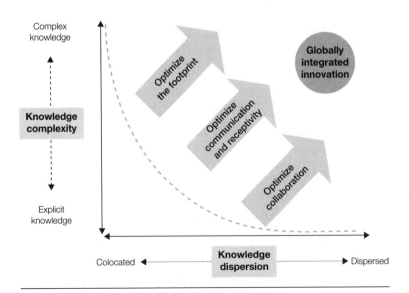

innovation, but it does provide executives and managers with practical guidance on some of the most critical activities they can initiate in the coming weeks and months.

Optimizing the Innovation Footprint

1. Identifying Knowledge Requirements

Understanding what knowledge is needed for innovation and where it is located is a key building block, because an optimized footprint should provide access to critical complex knowledge. Follow these steps to identify those requirements:

- Establish a working group of people from a wide range of different functions, businesses, and geographies to identify where the knowledge for innovation is located. The greater the diversity of people involved in this process, the richer the resulting knowledge map.

- Think in terms of not only the geographic location of knowledge, but also whether there are distinct holders of the knowledge (such as other companies, research institutes, public-sector entities, and so on). Locate each knowledge element identified through this process on the knowledge mapping tool in figure 3-2.

- Classify the knowledge to distinguish explicit, embedded, and complex knowledge. Establish alternative approaches to bricks-and-mortar sites such as attracting and foraying to access the explicit and embedded knowledge.

2. Reconfiguring or Building an Innovation Network

Undertake a knowledge and competency audit of every site in order to identify duplication and redundancy and create the knowledge maps that will indicate the optimal innovation footprint. Achieving an optimal footprint involves understanding not only where your company should be located but how big the network should be:

- Carry out a knowledge audit of the current innovation network by identifying the knowledge, skills, and capabilities at each site. Don't overlook the sites' relationships with external entities and partners as potentially valuable knowledge.

- To understand whether sites are making a differentiated contribution or not requires plotting the knowledge at each site on the knowledge mapping tool. This indicates the overall effectiveness of the current innovation footprint; the more gaps, duplications, and redundancy, the greater the degree of reconfiguration required.

- Map knowledge networks to identify gatekeepers of tacit knowledge. A simple way to do this is to ask a range of people in different roles, functions, and geographies, "Who do you talk to when you encounter a problem?" Just because a site as a whole may not make a unique contribution, it doesn't mean that it isn't home to valuable tacit knowledge.

- Based on the gaps between knowledge requirements and the current network, identify the locations of the sources of this missing knowledge: investigate the potential in harbinger locations, rapid cycle learning environments, favorable regulatory regimes, and partners.

- Assess existing operational subsidiaries, investigating their potential to expand their role and add value to innovation. What skills and unique knowledge can they leverage? Can they access local ecosystems or local partners?

- While the auditing and mapping processes are under way, review the optimal size of your innovation footprint based on your firm's legacy, culture, strategy, capabilities, and the knowledge dispersion in your industry.

- Investigate the various possibilities for attracting explicit knowledge. Talk to knowledge intermediaries about their services for "focused attracting" to solve problems and fill specific knowledge gaps. Assign the innovation organization the task of defining useful areas for "broad attracting" and creating a portal to promote this.

Optimizing Receptivity and Communication

3. Building Communication Networks

Without common and effective communication tools and mechanisms, dispersed teams will be unable to share knowledge and work as an integrated whole. So we suggest taking the following steps:

- Frequently, acquisitions and devolved purchasing decisions have left a legacy of incompatible systems. Undertake an audit of existing processes, tools, and systems across the network and identify areas where harmonization and commonality are lacking.

- Use the knowledge gatekeepers to help identify areas of common interest and complementary expertise that can be used to connect people and build problem-solving networks across distance and different environments.

- Commission a review of all knowledge databases within the global innovation organization, looking at how often they are used and by whom. Investigate how the most valuable and useful information from them can be captured in universal workflow systems.

4. Developing Cosmopolitan Managers

Managers with the skills to work in multiple different contexts are a rare but incredibly valuable asset. They act as bridges for the transfer of important complex knowledge and, as our survey showed, they perform well in dispersed teams and have a greater ability to absorb, interpret, and utilize new knowledge. Developing this type of cosmopolitan manager is vital for successful global innovation and requires the following:

- With the support of the HR function, explore the opportunity for benchmarking the recruitment, training, and career planning of cosmopolitan managers at companies with strong international manager programs and even diplomatic services. Sketch out plans for assignments that build knowledge and skills. Investigate reward structures that go beyond remuneration to include fast-track promotions, representation on high-level committees, and so on.

- Run an internal campaign to identify and attract bicultural people whose natural skills can be leveraged for integrating dispersed knowledge.

- Set up a program of onsite assignments and visits between sites to expose as many innovation staff as possible to different environments, locations, and contexts. Executives and managers who are used to jet-setting may forget that many innovation staff have never left their home country in a professional capacity. This program will also aid communication by building informal networks.

5. Culture Change and Building Trust

Building a culture of receptivity and trust is much more difficult to achieve than some of the other action points, as these elements come together over time and through practice:

- Ensure that senior managers visibly back and commit to culture changes.

- Launch a range of small projects and initiatives that deliver quantifiable benefits to staff and businesses to drive change in perceptions and behavior.

- Build an environment of transparency and open dialogue to explore assumptions and common ground and build trust between different parts of the firm. Some trust will come from site visits, assignments, small dispersed projects, and dispersed problem-solving initiatives.

Optimizing Collaboration

6. Managing Global Projects

Global innovation projects ultimately leverage the optimized footprint and enhanced communication capabilities to deliver innovative products, services, or business models. Building a competence in global projects takes time, so it's important to begin the process soon by building the structures and introducing the processes and mechanisms needed:

- Establish a multisite, multifunctional working group to roll out the global project frameworks discussed in chapter 6. In particular:

  - Use the knowledge maps drawn up as part of optimizing the footprint to identify where capabilities are located for projects.

  - Begin to build the trust and competencies needed for large, complex, global projects with small dispersed projects.

  - Identify a set of critical and trusted subcontractors and bring them into the process of competence building through small projects.

- Begin the process of building a strong global project management organization made up of talented, experienced people from different cultures and different functions. This assignment should be aspirational, providing valuable experience and exposure by working closely with senior managers involved in project decision making.

7. Collaborative Innovation with Partners

Collaborating with partners is already becoming a common feature of innovation and, in many instances, is the only way of accessing the required knowledge. Adopting a structured approach to collaboration not only supports the innovation process but reduces the risks inherent in working with partners:

- Encourage different parts of the innovation organization to engage in dialogues with a wide range of partners to identify opportunities. It's important to put a process in place to capture these conversations and bring them together, because each could provide a fragment of a potential innovation.

- Use the gaps highlighted in the knowledge maps (created as part of optimizing the footprint) to identify and select potential partners that can provide the requisite knowledge and capabilities and bring diversity to collaborations.

- To support partner selection, introduce a process to vet potential partners along the seven dimensions of capabilities, cospecialization, contribution, commitment, credibility, compatibility, and strategy.

Based on some of the remarkable things we have seen companies achieve during the course of our research, we believe that by implementing the lessons and frameworks from the previous chapters, every company can build and manage a globally integrated innovation capability. There is, however, one caveat. Senior management vision and commitment alone will not be enough to drive this transformation. Too often, firms fail to implement strategic change simply because of a lack of buy-in from groups of middle managers who either are happy with the status quo or are unaware of the need and rationale for change. Successfully implementing the changes we have outlined depends on gaining the allegiance and enthusiasm of the entire innovation organization by openly discussing the threats and challenges, engaging in dialogues about what changes are needed, and being inclusive in the implementation of those changes.

Moving toward a new model of global innovation may be challenging, but that doesn't make it any less urgent. The competitive landscape is rapidly changing, so what made companies successful innovators in the past won't continue to do so in the future. Companies that don't embrace this change and the opportunities it affords will find the twenty-first century a difficult place in which to compete. Those that do will find the globally integrated approach a rewarding, effective way to innovate.

The Nature of Innovation Is Changing

Innovation can no longer be the preserve of the traditional notion of science- and technology-based invention or new knowledge creation. This model, dominant during the twentieth century, is being replaced by the concept of innovation as bringing together existing knowledge and combining it to create something new.[1] When innovation was framed on the Edison or Marconi model of product invention, there was an underlying assumption that improvement equated to technology advancement.[2]

The Scope of Innovation Is Broader

Today, innovation is about new services, value propositions, and business models. Pioneering medical services in India, for example, have radically reduced the costs and improved the quality of cardiac and cataract surgery, not through the introduction of breakthrough technologies, but by reorganizing activity systems.[3] And, although they may not be some of the world's favorite airlines, the new business models adopted by low-cost carriers has made them some of the world's largest and most profitable.

At the same time, the notion that innovations that are still technology-based have to be leading-edge is no longer true. The most successful and widely adopted innovations aren't always the ones pursuing ever greater functionality. One of the biggest success stories in mobile telecoms over the past decade wasn't the much hyped (and extremely costly to providers) 3G platform, which offered leading-edge mobile Internet services. It was a very simple and crude data service called SMS, or text messaging, that captured people's imagination and had a radical impact on the way we communicate.

Lead Markets Are Changing

Traditionally, new products, solutions, and business models have been pioneered in a company's home market, which was also assumed to be the lead market. These were then sold across other developed markets (with any practical, market-specific adaptations made along the way). As a consumer class with sufficient purchasing power emerged in other markets, the innovations would then cascade down to these distant and different places. By the late 1980s, it was already clear that significant opportunities lay outside companies' lead or home markets and that the transnational organizational model offered a solution to leverage different markets.[4]

Christopher Bartlett and Sumantra Ghoshal described the transnational as a multibusiness company with multiple home countries, each of which essentially provided home-country comparative advantage. So, for example, the telecom equipment transnational Alcatel ran its worldwide underwater cables business from Norway because, with its many fjords, Norway was an early lead market for underwater cables. Ericsson ran its shipboard communications business from the Netherlands, because its long history of seafaring meant that better market knowledge and skills were available there than in Sweden. These multiple home markets transferred or projected knowledge to other subsidiaries that played an implementer role in other countries. With a few exceptions, such as Unilever in India and Heineken in Africa, when Bartlett and Ghoshal did their research, the dominant innovation perspective was still essentially triadic. In other words, innovative capability wasn't expected outside of three regions—the United States, Europe, and Japan.

Now, however, the triad is losing its dominance, and home markets are no longer necessarily lead markets. This means that the innovation activities of many Western companies must break free of their geographical roots. Successful innovations can originate by addressing unmet consumer needs in distant and different markets, so there is a strong imperative to learn from tomorrow's potential lead markets, as well as current ones, and combine that knowledge to create global innovations.

Innovating in New Markets: Reverse Innovation

The more recent argument for reverse innovation challenges the preeminence of the triadic developed markets by extending the transnational model to home bases in emerging countries.[5]

Here, low per capita incomes provide a stimulus to achieving cost-reduction breakthroughs both in process and the resulting product or service. Products born from reverse engineering can sometimes find markets in developed economies either by appealing to less affluent consumers or by including features that make them attractive in different segments. More importantly, innovations from emerging markets may be competitively disruptive in developed economies, offering alternatives good enough to take market share away from incumbents. Witness the success of Korean cars in the United States and, more recently, Dacia vehicles in Europe: the Dacia Logan, Renault's low-cost, no-frills, €6,000 car, launched in 2004, was designed for emerging markets. Its simpler parts, minimal electronic functions, and high suspension were designed for potholes and rough roads. However, Renault found a strong market for this vehicle in Europe where cash-strapped customers were attracted to not only the low purchase price but lower maintenance and repair costs. In 2010, only five years after its launch in Western Europe, Dacia accounted for 1.7 percent of new car sales in the region, with annual sales of over seventy-five thousand in France and twenty-four thousand in Germany alone.

While the extended transnational logic of reverse innovation is compelling, it doesn't address the challenges of global innovation. What it does do is advocate a market-driven perspective in which firms widen their innovation activities to include demanding emerging markets, then export the resulting innovations in order to preempt competition from other firms in those markets. But managing global innovation is an order of magnitude more complex than performing reverse, but essentially local, innovation. Global innovation is about accessing unique and differentiated skills and capabilities from all over the world and bringing them together in innovations.

Take the example of the global development of GE's wind turbines. The design and integration work is done in Niskayuna, upstate New York. A lab in Shanghai designs the microprocessors that control the pitch of the blades, engineers in Bangalore build mathematical models to maximize the efficiency of materials in the turbine, and a team in Munich, in close collaboration with the Technical University of Munich, has designed a system that calculates optimal wing pitch at any given time to produce maximum electricity. That is global innovation at its most effective.

Thinking About the Customer: User-Driven Innovation

The idea that innovation can be driven by user requirements isn't a new one. In the mid-1970s, MIT professor Eric von Hippel identified the dominant role that users played in the development of new scientific instruments.[6] Over the following years, much attention was given to the contribution that "lead customers" could make to the innovation process through their insight and suggestions about emerging trends and their own future requirements. But until the dot-com revolution, most of this interest was focused on the user as another business and not the ultimate end user.[7]

The role of the end user as a partner in innovation started to take hold at the end of the 1990s, as companies like Amazon, Dell, and Microsoft began co-opting customers to improve and personalize their offerings.[8] As opposed to mass customization, in which all the variants of choice open to the customer are defined by the firm, user-driven innovation has been evolving in recent years to focus on understanding latent customer requirements. Nowhere is this better seen than in the ethnographic-based approaches many companies are employing to unearth solutions for hitherto overlooked customers in emerging markets.

Collaboration: Ecosystem and Open Innovation

Finally, innovation increasingly relies on collaborating with a range of partners in ecosystems. In most industries, the days when all innovation could be undertaken entirely in-house are long gone. As the boundaries between different industries become more porous, individual firms simply don't have all of the knowledge and capabilities needed for innovation. Also, as the cost of innovation increases along with higher levels of related risk, the necessity for collaborative innovation with external partners increases.

One particular form of collaboration that has received a lot of attention over recent years is open innovation, in which firms seek knowledge from external players and also make their own unused knowledge available to other companies.[9] The proponents of open innovation are companies like Procter & Gamble and Eli Lilly that have a strong technology or scientific component in their products. The knowledge they seek in open innovation marketplaces tends to be well codified and not new.

Although the idea of open innovation is compelling, more and more firms are finding it fraught with difficulties. First, IP rights are not well regulated, leaving many companies in a situation where they give away more than they receive. In any badly regulated market where price is a poor indicator of the real value of a transaction, there will be free riders. Second, open innovation is limited to dealing with highly codified knowledge. Any knowledge more complex requires a degree of physical proximity that open innovation practices can't provide. Finally, open innovation lacks a form of legitimate governance. This is currently an issue in the ICT industries with interactions among platforms, application developers, and value-adding resellers. But as more industries experiment by opening up their innovation to a wider range of external entities, they too will find it increasingly difficult to create and apportion value without stringent forms of governance in place.

While collaborative innovation, organized around deliberately formed ecosystems and communities, is an inevitable and promising way forward, our prognosis on the future and potential value created by a widely adopted approach to open innovation is more reserved. Open innovation does have a role to play in global innovation, but, as we outlined in chapter 2, it's a small part of the solution (specifically for codified knowledge) and not the complete answer.

Knowledge Is Increasingly Dispersed

Most of the knowledge needed for innovation could once be found in or close to a company's primary markets. Now it is increasingly dispersed and diverse. Among the many forces driving this knowledge dispersion, we have identified five radical shifts that occurred progressively over the past three decades or are currently under way, and have led to greater knowledge diffusion and diversity: (1) globalization and the opening of new consumer markets; (2) increasing technological complexity and convergence; (3) demographic changes; (4) greater external pressures and, in particular, environmental concerns; and (5) offshore outposts and outsourcing.

New Consumer Markets

India and China are rarely out of the business news these days. Even before recession stalled the prospects of growth in many developed markets, India and China's burgeoning economies were promising swaths of new customers at a time when commoditization and saturation had become the bywords for many industries in their traditional markets.

Together, Brazil, Russia, India and China (the BRIC countries) have populations of around 3 billion. Their average annual GDP growth rate between 2006 and 2010 was 6.9 percent (with India and China posting an impressive 9.8 percent over the period), and they were the first economies to bounce back from the financial and economic crises of 2008.[1] Even before the rest of the world's emerging markets are added to the BRIC giants, the benefits of innovating at the "bottom of the pyramid" become clear.[2] To do this requires accessing local knowledge in order to understand unmet consumer needs and local constraints and not merely paring back and adapting existing product ranges to try and attain a suitable price point.

The opening of new markets not only provides the opportunity to learn from the world and access diffuse and differentiated customer knowledge for innovation.[3] It also ushers in a new threat in the form of ambitious and hungry local players who have the advantage of understanding their local markets. In recent years, they have leveraged local and foreign talent via in-house development, licensing, and acquisitions to access and develop technical competencies equal to, and in some cases ahead of, their multinational competitors. Fifteen years ago, it was unknown, but today, China's Huawei is among the world's leading telecom equipment makers. India's Wipro is the world's largest R&D services provider (and is listed on the New York Stock Exchange). Companies that fail to get an innovation foothold in the new consumer markets are effectively sanctioning their own demise. To compete successfully against these new players both in their home markets and on the global stage, companies need to access the same vital market and customer knowledge, while at the same time leverage their global network, assets, and processes to create a pipeline of innovations that combines the best technologies with the most relevant consumer insights from around the world.

Increasing Technology Complexity and Industry Convergence

Competencies that have been built up over years of specialization are now only part of what is required to develop current and next-generation products, services, and business models. This is forcing companies to seek the new knowledge they are lacking from a wider geographic canvas and away from their traditional hubs. Compare a car built in the 1960s with one built in 2012. Body aside, the former was essentially a triumph of mechanical engineering. In terms of technologies, it was relatively simple and had changed little from the earliest models that rolled off Ford's production lines in the early 1900s. The modern car, on the other hand, is a very different proposition. From the early 1990s, there has been a rapid increase in the number of electromechanical and electronic elements in cars in the power train, chassis, body, and interiors. A new car today can contain as many as two hundred sensors, over sixty microprocessors, and up to a hundred eighty software-driven functions; and many of these are developed in India and China, far away from Detroit, Germany, and Japan.

And it isn't just the auto industry facing this shift. Industry convergence has challenged many industries to extend their capabilities into previously unchartered territories as the boundaries between industries, or rather their underlying knowledge bases, blur. From mobile telecoms to health care, a battle is currently being waged to control the choke points in the value chain. Accessing new diverse and dispersed knowledge is no longer the preserve of a few cutting-edge firms, but essential for any company hoping to remain competitive as its industry reshapes.

Innovation Needs to Follow the Brains

The emergence of new knowledge hot spots is now gathering pace due to the biggest demographic changes in modern history. As the baby boom generation heads toward retirement, the number of people leaving the workforce in a short time is unprecedented. According to the UN, between 2010 and 2050, the number of people over age sixty will increase globally from 759 million to over 2 billion, with 33 percent of the population in the developed world of retirement age, up from around 20 percent in 2008.[4] The loss of so many experienced people in such a short time could have serious implications for an organization's innovative capabilities. Those employees are the guardians of complex knowledge, and without them, deep competency holes can appear. This problem is exacerbated by the fact that the developed world hasn't produced enough science and engineering graduates to replace those retiring, and it could not have done so with birthrates continually on the decline since the 1960s.

For various reasons, it's very difficult to compare accurately the number of science, engineering, and technology (SET) students graduating in different countries. Countries aggregate data in different ways, and in addition, the timeliness of published data varies dramatically. What is clear, however, is that while the general growth in the annual number of SET graduates has slowed dramatically in the developed world, it is surging ahead elsewhere. For example, in the four years to 2008 (the latest available data), the United States saw a 3 percent rise in the number of SET graduates, to almost 250,000 annually.[5] In contrast, the number of SET graduates in China grew by almost 43 percent over the same period and then increased by an additional 9 percent over the following two years to just over 800,000.[6] And in India, the number of SET graduates grew 27 percent from 2008 to 2010 to 497,500.[7]

At the undergraduate level, there can be huge differences in the quality of graduates from different institutions in different countries, making true comparisons of available talent difficult. However, in 2009, 22 percent of PhDs awarded by U.S. universities went to students from emerging economies (up from 13.7 percent a decade previously), with 13 percent of the total awarded to Chinese and Indian nationals.[8] With tighter restrictions on working visas for foreigners in the United States, combined with booming economies back home, greater numbers of these U.S.-educated PhDs are returning to India and China.

Clearly, in terms of sheer numbers, the balance of brainpower is shifting eastward. Innovation footprints need to reflect this shift.

Growing External Pressures

External factors such as environmental threats, regulations, and standards play a part in the diffusion of critical knowledge in many industries. The looming demise of the oil industry coupled with growing demands for sustainability, for example, is forcing firms in an entire raft of related sectors, including utilities companies and the auto industry, to look for alternative sources of energy and power, from wave technology to hydrogen cells. These innovative new technologies are emerging in new hot spots around the world.

Regulations, for example, can have a big impact on where knowledge is able to develop. Perhaps in no sector has the contrast between a lenient and stringent regulatory approach been starker than in early days of mobile telecoms. Despite the fact that many of the early key technological breakthroughs came from the United States, the Federal Communications Commission wouldn't allocate the spectrum needed for a consumer cellular market and didn't authorize the first commercial cellular service until 1982. This stymied local players. With the regulator effectively preventing the development of a consumer market, there was little incentive to invest in innovation. In contrast, supportive regulatory regimes meant that the first Nordic-wide service was up and running by the late 1970s and Japan's first commercial service was launched in 1979. The Nordic model was then adopted throughout Europe for the creation and regulation of GSM services, paving the way for Ericsson, Nokia, and Alcatel to take leading roles in the telecom industry.

Offshore Outposts and Outsourcing

What initially began as a low-cost approach to manufacturing, either by outsourcing to a third party or establishing a subsidiary in a low-cost location has, over time, led to the migration of certain knowledge and capabilities away from traditional hubs to offshore locations. In both scenarios, the offshore manufacturing site gradually moved up the value chain as firms sought the cost benefits of relocating noncritical support, development, and testing capabilities to offshore outsourcing companies or in-house subsidiaries, primarily in emerging economies. As these offshore sites grew in breadth and experience, it was inevitable that they would develop leading-edge knowledge and skills in their specialist domains (knowledge no longer possessed by the Western multinationals' innovation hubs). In addition, entire ecosystems of local suppliers and partners have emerged to support innovation in these locations.

A clear example of knowledge dispersion brought about through offshore outsourcing can be seen in the mobile phone handset sector. Beginning in the late 1990s, in a bid to cut costs, many handset firms outsourced the manufacture of their phones to Taiwanese electronics companies. The experience and capabilities built up in Taiwan made it a leading knowledge center. One of the companies that typifies that transition from original equipment manufacturer to innovative giant is HTC. Founded in 1997, the firm began by manufacturing Microsoft-based PDAs and quickly became an expert in designing Microsoft-based devices. In 2002, it started designing phones for telecom operators worldwide. This gave HTC unique insight into consumer and market demands. After accumulating a huge amount of technical knowledge and market insight, four years later it launched its own brand of innovative smartphones.[9] By 2011, HTC had become the world's third-largest handset maker by market value and had won many awards for its innovative products.

Similarly, in the 1980s, Singapore was largely a low-cost manufacturing center. But over time, companies such as HP took advantage of its well-educated, English-speaking workforce, delegating more design and innovation work to subsidiaries based there. Today, Singapore is one the world's leading centers for knowledge in fields as diverse as biology, communications, and logistics.

NOTES

Preface

1. S. J. Palmisano, "The Globally Integrated Enterprise," *Foreign Affairs* 85, no. 3 (2006): 127–136.

2. Y. Doz, J. Santos, and P. Williamson, *From Global to Metanational: How Companies Win in the Knowledge Economy* (Boston: Harvard Business School Press, 2001).

3. Y. Doz, K. Wilson, S. Veldhoen, and T. Goldbrunner, "Innovation: Is Global the Way Forward?" Booz Allen Hamilton and INSEAD, 2006.

Chapter One

1. For a more detailed description of the evolution of Tata Communications, see P. J. Williamson and K. Wilson, "Tata Communications Ltd.: Innovating a Global Business Model," case study (Cambridge, UK: University of Cambridge, Judge Business School, 2012).

2. Although the survey was published in 2006, we strongly believe the results remain relevant. More recent surveys and published work examining the internationalization of innovation have concurred with our findings. Also, anecdotal evidence from companies points to the currency of our findings. See Y. Doz, K. Wilson, S. Veldhoen, and T. Goldbrunner, "Innovation: Is Global the Way Forward?" Booz Allen Hamilton and INSEAD, 2006.

3. See UNCTAD 2005, "World Investment Report"; BCG, "Innovation 2006"; B. Jaruzelski and K. Dehoff, "Beyond Borders: Global Innovation 1000," Booz & Company, 2008.

4. Ibid.

5. C. Mackay, *Extraordinary Popular Delusions and the Madness of Crowds* (London, Wordsworth Editions, 1995; London: Richard Bentley London, 1841).

6. A. H. Maslow, "A Theory of Human Motivation," *Psychological Review* 50, no. 4 (July 1943): 370–396.

7. P. Williamson and M. Zeng, "Value-for-Money Strategies for Recessionary Times," *Harvard Business Review*, March 2009, 66.

Chapter Two

1. D. Farrell and A. J. Grant, "China's Looming Talent Shortage," *McKinsey Quarterly* no. 4 (November 2005): 70.

2. W. Kuemmerle, "Building Effective R&D Capabilities Abroad," *Harvard Business Review*, March–April 1997, 61.

3. P. Williamson and M. Zeng, "Value-for-Money Strategies for Recessionary Times," *Harvard Business Review*, March 2009, 66.

4. C. K. Prahalad, *The Fortune at the Bottom of the Pyramid: Eradicating Poverty Through Profits* (Upper Saddle River, NJ: Prentice Hall, 2006).

5. The ISU was founded in 1987 at MIT. The intention behind it was to create an international, intercultural, and interdisciplinary institute to focus on all aspects of space science. In addition to postgraduate courses, it holds annual summer sessions (in a different country each year) to bring together professionals from industry and academia. In 2002, the ISU inaugurated a permanent campus in Strasbourg. To date, it has 1,800 alumni.

6. H. W. Chesbrough, *Open Innovation: The New Imperative for Creating and Profiting from Technology* (Boston: Harvard Business School Press, 2003).

Chapter Three

1. For more on innovation in emerging markets at GE Healthcare, see J. Singh, "GE Healthcare (A): Innovating for Emerging Markets," Case 311-048-1 (Fontainebleau, France: INSEAD, 2011).

2. J. Donne, "Meditation XVII: Devotions upon Emergent Occasions," 1624, reprinted in *The Complete English Poems* (London: Penguin Books, 1996).

3. M. Y. Zhang and B. W. Stening, *China 2.0 The Transformation of an Emerging Superpower . . . And the New Opportunities* (Singapore: John Wiley & Sons [Asia] Pte. Ltd., 2010).

4. C. K. Prahalad, *The Fortune at the Bottom of the Pyramid: Eradicating Poverty Through Profits* (Upper Saddle River, NJ: Prentice Hall, 2006).

5. D. Bayles and T. Orland, *Art & Fear: Observations on the Perils (and Rewards) of Artmaking* (Eugene, OR: Image Continuum Press, 1993).

6. Y. Doz and M. Hunter, "Fuji Xerox and the Xerox Corp: Turning Tables?," Case 303-076-1 (Fontainebleau, France: INSEAD, 2003).

Chapter Four

1. M. Reynolds, A. Cave, and I. Bettles, "Design Gets Six Appeal from Team-Based Event," *Electronics Weekly* 2.5.3004, no. 2085 (2003): 22.

2. See E. P. Spencer, "EuroDisney: What Happened? What Next?" *Journal of International Marketing* 3, no. 3 (1995): 103–114; A. Ettienne-Benz, M. Bertoneche, and F. Leonard, "Disneyland Paris, Case Study on Global Strategy for International Set-up, Marketing, Finance and Set-up, 'Mickey Mouse' or an American Mouse in France," Case 396-051-1 (Fontainebleau, France: INSEAD, 1996); and D. Gayatry and T. Phani Madhay, "Euro Disney: Failed Americanism?" Case 304-557-1 (Hyderabad, India: IBS Case Development Center, 2004).

Chapter Five

1. J. S. Brown and P. Duguid, "Organizational Learning and Communities of Practice: Towards a Unified View of Working, Learning and Innovation," *Organisation Science* 2, no. 1 (1991): 40–57; and J. A. Swan, H. Scarbrough, and M. Robertson, "The Construction of Communities of Practice in the Management of Innovation," *Management Learning* 33, no. 4 (2002): 477–497.

2. Ibid.

3. T. J. Allen, *Managing the Flow of Technology: Technology Transfer and the Dissemination of Technological Information Within the R&D Organization* (Cambridge, MA: MIT Press, 1977).

4. M. Y. Brannen and Y. Doz, "Corporate Languages and Strategic Agility," *California Management Review*, Spring 2012.

5. T. Khanna, J. Song, and K. Lee, "The Paradox of Samsung's Rise," *Harvard Business Review*, July–August 2011, 142–147.

6. See S. Newell, G. David, and D. Chand, "An Analysis of Trust Among Globally Distributed Work Teams in an Organizational Setting," *Knowledge and Process Management* 14, no. 3 (2007): 158–168; M. Serva, M. Fuller, and R. Mayer, "The Reciprocal Nature of Trust: A Longitudinal Study of Interacting Teams," *Journal of Organizational Behavior* 26, no. 6 (2005): 625–648; and M. Mortensen and T. Beyene, "Firsthand Experience

and the Subsequent Role of Reflected Knowledge in Cultivating Trust in Global Collaboration," working paper 09-131, Harvard Business School, Boston, 2009.

Chapter Six

1. For more on trust, see: S. L. Jarvenpaa and D. E. Leidner, "Communication and Trust in Global Virtual Teams," *Organization Science* 10, no. 6 (1999): 791–815; D. L. Ferrin, K. T. Dirks, and P. P. Shah, "Direct and Indirect Effects of Third-Party Relationships on Interpersonal Trust," *Journal of Applied Psychology* 91, no. 4 (2006): 870–883; D. McKnight et al., "Initial Trust Formation in New Organizational Relationships," *Academy of Management Review* 23, no. 3 (1998): 473–490; P. M. Doney, J. P. Cannon, and M. R. Mullen, "Understanding the Influence of National Culture on the Development of Trust," *Academy of Management Review* 23, no. 3 (1998): 601–620.

2. D. Dvir, T. Raz, and A. J. Shenhar, "An Empirical Analysis of the Relationship Between Project Planning and Project Success," *International Journal of Project Management* 21, no. 2 (2003): 89–95.

3. C. D. Cramton, "The Mutual Knowledge Problem and Its Consequences for Dispersed Collaboration," *Organization Science* 12, no. 3 (2001): 346–371.

4. L. Argote. and E. Miron-Spektor, "Organizational Learning: From Experience to Knowledge," *Organization Science* 22, no. 5 (2011): 1123–1138; K. Lewis, D. Lange, and L. Gillis, "Transactive Memory Systems, Learning, and Learning Transfer," *Organization Science* 16, no. 6 (2005): 581–598; and J. A. Espinosa et al., "Familiarity, Complexity, and Team Performance in Geographically Distributed Software Development," *Organization Science* 18, no. 4 (2007): 613–630.

5. For more on the importance of project manager flexibility, see A. De Meyer, C. Loch, and M. Pich, "Managing Project Uncertainty: From Variation to Chaos," *MIT Sloan Management Review*, Winter 2002, 60.

Chapter Seven

1. For more information, see D. Schifrin, M. LaBrecque, and R. Burgelman, "Intel and WiMax in 2010," Case SM-179 (Palo Alto, CA: Stanford Graduate School of Business, 2010).

Appendix One

1. J. Lave and E. Wenger, *Situated Learning: Legitimate Peripheral Participation* (Cambridge, UK: Cambridge University Press, 1991).

2. R. S. Rosenbloom and W. J. Spencer, eds., *Engines of Innovation: US Industrial Research at the End of an Era* (Boston: Harvard Business School Press, 1996); M. B. W. Graham, "Corporate Research and Development: The Latest Transformation," *Technology in Society* 7, (1985): 179–195.

3. C. K. Prahalad, "The Innovation Sandbox," *Strategy + Business* 44 (2006).

4. C. A. Bartlett and S. Ghoshal, *Managing Across Boarders: The Transnational Solution* (Boston: Harvard Business School Press, 1989).

5. V. Govindarajan and R. Ramamurti, "Reverse Innovation, Emerging Markets, and Global Strategy," *Global Strategy Journal* 1 (2011): 191–205.

6. E. von Hippel, "The Dominant Role of Users in the Scientific Instrument Innovation Process," *Research Policy* 5, no. 3 (1976): 212–239.

7. E. von Hippel, "Successful Industrial Products from Customer Ideas: Presentation of a New Customer-Active Paradigm with Evidence and Implications," *Journal of Marketing* 42, no. 1 (1978): 39–49; and S. Thomke and E. von Hippel, "Customers as Innovators: A New Way to Create Value," *Harvard Business Review* 80, no. 4 (2002): 81.

8. C. K. Prahalad and V. Ramaswamy, "Co-opting Customer Competence," *Harvard Business Review*, January–February 2000, 79.

9. H. W. Chesbrough, *Open Innovation: The New Imperative for Creating and Profiting from Technology* (Boston: Harvard Business School Press, 2003).

Appendix Two

1. Calculated based on World Bank data from http://data.world bank.org.

2. C. K. Prahalad, *The Fortune at the Bottom of the Pyramid: Eradicating Poverty Through Profits* (Upper Saddle River, NJ: Prentice Hall, 2006).

3. Y. Doz, J. Santos, and P. Williamson, *From Global to Metanational: How Companies Win in the Knowledge Economy* (Boston: Harvard Business School Press, 2001).

4. United Nations, *World Population Prospects: The 2008 Revision*, http://esa.un.org/unpp/.

5. Calculated from National Science Foundation statistics, http:// www.nsf.gov/statistics/.

6. Calculated based on data from China's Ministry of Education, www. moe.edu.cn.

7. Calculated based on estimated data supplied by NASSCOM, http:// www.nasscom.org/.

8. Calculated from statistics collated by the U.S. National Science Foundation.

9. F-H. Liu, L-J. Chen, and H. H. Chen, "Sustaining Client Relationships in the Contract Manufacturer Own-Brand Building Process: The Case of a Smartphone Firm," *International Journal of Business and Management* 6, no. 7 (2011): 59–68.

INDEX

knowledge complexity and, 8,
9–10
learning in, 177–179
legitimate purpose for, 114
at Novartis, 73–74
open innovation in, 175–176,
216–217
optimizing, 207–210
partner selection for, 176–182
practice in, 122–123
quantity versus quality and, 75
stages of, 172–173
at Tata Communications, 11
value creation in, 180–181
colocation
knowledge complexity and, 5–10
with manufacturing, 18
physical versus virtual sites and,
25–26
with research institutions, 174
commitment
aligning among partners,
181–182
to global projects, 141, 142,
164–165
of managers, 63, 207
of partners, 187–189
communication
across contexts, 119–123
barriers to optimizing,
94–103
in collaboration, 174–175
of complex knowledge, 8–9
connecting nodes for, 111–112,
115–118
in global projects, 144, 146–147,
151–152, 158–159, 169
inadequate connections in,
96–99
management and, 110

optimizing, 205–207
people versus technology in, 110,
111–118
proximity and, 117
receptivity and, 107–135
receptivity barriers and,
103–105
at Siemens, 120–122
trust building and, 151–152
communities of practice (CoPs),
113–115, 134
competence-based resource allocation, 154–158
competence development paths, 81
competition, 104, 200
complementarity value, 57, 58,
66–70, 88
boundaries and, 70
collaboration and, 69
at GE, 63
optimal proportion of, 60
partners and, 186
summary of, 77
complementary knowledge,
51, 52
complex knowledge
accessing, 35
communicating, 95–97
competitive advantage of,
139–140
definition of, 34–35
dispersion of, 5–10
experiencing approach with, 35,
36–41
industry sector differences in, 15
conflict, 146, 165
connect-and-develop strategy, 48
consensus, 159
constraints, capability, 85
consumer knowledge, 19

ABOUT THE AUTHORS

Yves L. Doz is the Solvay Chaired Professor of Technological Innovation at INSEAD and a professor of strategic management. For many years, one of his key priorities has been to improve the performance of multinational companies and their usefulness to society—through research, consulting, and teaching. He has written many articles and books on these issues, in particular *The Multinational Mission*, coauthored with C. K. Prahalad, and *From Global to Metanational*, with INSEAD colleagues José Santos and Peter Williamson.

Keeley Wilson worked in banking and strategy consulting in Europe and Northeast Asia before joining INSEAD in 1999. Three years later, she began working with Yves Doz. Her research projects at INSEAD have focused on innovation strategies across a range of industrial sectors, the challenges of managing global projects, and establishing and integrating innovation centers in China and India. She has worked with a wide range of global companies, helping them implement new tools and processes to support business model migration, manage strategic alliances, and build a wide range of global innovation capabilities.